PLANNING THE NEW SUBURBIA

Flexibility by Design

PLANNING THE NEW SUBURBIA

Flexibility by Design

Avi Friedman

with

David Krawitz

Maged Senbel

Doug Raphael

Jennifer E. Steffel

Jasmin S. Fréchette

John Watt

UBCPress · Vancouver · Toronto

Printed in Canada on acid-free paper

National Library of Canada Cataloguing in Publication Data

Friedman, Avi, 1952-
  Planning the new suburbia

  Includes bibliographical references and index.
  ISBN 0-7748-0858-6 (bound); ISBN 0-7748-0859-4 (pbk.)

  1. Suburbs. 2. Suburbs – Case studies. 3. City planning.
4. Community development, Urban. I. Title.

HT351.F74 2001   307.74   C2001-911418-4

This book has been published with the help of a grant from the Humanities and Social Sciences Federation of Canada, using funds provided by the Social Sciences and Humanities Research Council of Canada.

UBC Press acknowledges the financial support of the Government of Canada through the Book Publishing Industry Development Program (BPIDP) for our publishing activities.

Canadä

We also gratefully acknowledge the support of the Canada Council for the Arts for our publishing program, as well as the support of the British Columbia Arts Council.

UBC Press
The University of British Columbia
2029 West Mall, Vancouver, BC V6T 1Z2
(604) 822-5959
Fax: (604) 822-6083
E-mail: info@ubcpress.ca
www.ubcpress.ca

Contents

In the thousands of years that people have lived in organized settlements, they have constantly manipulated the environment that surrounds them to make it a more hospitable place to live. Homes, clusters of homes, and whole communities have evolved over time as a result of this natural process. Generations of dwellers have modified their homes gradually, as need arose, and eventually reshaped entire communities. Early transformations were, unsurprisingly, amorphous and unregulated; there existed no decrees as to how many or what kind of houses one could build, or as to what form of expansion an existing home could take. The laws that governed accretion were property boundaries, common sense, and the skill capacity of builders.

In the aftermath of the Industrial Revolution, society adopted a more complex civic structure, and the need to control and merge urban systems became evident. The design of a metropolis, and eventually a suburb in which residential and industrial uses could coexist and where transportation arteries brought the component parts of the development together, required planning and regulatory processes. These processes were manifested in control mechanisms that ensured that built form would adhere to a preconceived image or vision of the intended settlement. Zoning bylaws and building codes were some of the tools used to regulate development. Various methods of prior review by administrative bodies were also used. Naturally, these controls hampered the speed at which people could now alter their environment and the ultimate freedom they felt in doing so. When society and its members were slow to evolve, as was the case at the beginning of the twentieth century, the codes and the processes by which they were implemented made sense: they ensured a standard of building safety and a minimum level of sanitation where previously there were none. At the threshold of the twenty-first century, however, as social, technological, and environmental issues are becoming more complex and are changing rapidly, it appears that the planning processes that govern how society lives require revisiting. A new outlook that can encompass existing as well as new communities, in both urban and suburban contexts, is needed.

This book challenges established planning conventions and proposes a modified approach to the design and approval procedures of suburban development, one that recognizes its evolutionary nature. The new process includes codes that are flexible and that offer guidance at the beginning and throughout the life of a building project. The approach encourages and outlines an additive process of gradual, small-scale transformations that enable a neighbourhood to develop holistically.

The thrust of the book is preceded by three chapters intended to furnish the background necessary to fully grasp the concepts proposed and the context in which they were considered. The first chapter outlines the historical evolution of planning concepts. The second recounts how the "suburban ideal" has made such a dominant impression on North American social form. And the third chapter examines several precedent theories and projects of designing flexible suburban outgrowth.

Chapters 4 through 6 examine three situations, set in the context of residential developments, in which a new planning ideology is required. Each chapter begins by establishing a theoretical framework on which a later application case study is based. These case studies are set in real places and have been carried out under very realistic conditions.

The first situation to be examined, in Chapter 4, is the present-day stagnation of the postwar suburb. Now over a generation old, such suburbs are experiencing a rapid population turnover and, in some cases, societal decay, since homes, land uses, and the laws regulating them no longer accurately reflect what the North American population requires in order to carry on a fulfilling existence. The proposed intervention is an opportunity to add a new layer of suburban growth to the existing well-established layer. Such a solution is challenging; when dealing with existing communities, issues of design must be balanced with such concerns as property value fluctuations, existing community character, and the demands of the already-present residents.

The second situation to be examined is the contemporary, all-or-nothing practice of designing and receiving approval for construction of new, large-scale suburban development. It challenges the convention whereby a fully detailed master plan, specifying the most minute particulars, is prepared for a large plot, despite the fact that the realization of such a project may take a very long time. The alternative approach proposes a framework and guidelines within which segments of the whole could be designed and built by different development teams over the life of the project. Harmony and continuity would be maintained, yet the housing form could be adapted to the demands of the market. Ultimately, a more relevant, saleable housing and community form would result.

Chapter 6 deals with the attempt to infill a large parcel of vacant land within an established neighbourhood. In order to integrate the new development seamlessly with the existing one, architectural control mechanisms must be established that truly capture the essence and character of the existing community. Rather than being a mere replication of what is on site already, such an intervention would provide for the needs of the present, allow spatially and structurally for future change, and strongly address its context. In doing so, contemporary, flexible design solutions are integrated into an older environment without disruption of the suburban social fabric. It is hoped that such a new intervention would not only benefit its immediate residents but also serve as a nucleus around which a rejuvenation of the existing community could take place.

In articulating these three situations, it is hoped that some of the proposed concepts will be applied in actual practice, in spirit at least, if not in the true letter of what has been proposed. Implementing this methodology will bring the design, planning, and development professions towards a more appropriate, flexible product, and will enable society to pursue a more fulfilling way of life: living in the new suburbia, flexible by design.

This book is the outcome of a two-decade-long investigation into design flexibility in urban environments and housing. The second of these two decades, when I served as director of the Affordable Homes Program at the McGill School of Architecture, has been devoted to theoretical and practical experimentation. The housing design studio that I teach has provided me with an opportunity to reflect on these ideas.

I am grateful to the professors, urban planners, and architects who helped me guide and review these projects, and to the students who participated in them.

To Professors Norbert Schoenauer and John Archer and graduate students Amar Alnemer, Theresa Cheng, Jocelyn Duff, Susan Fisher, Shazia Nasir, Benjamin Sternthal, and Dorota Wlodarczyk-Karzynska, participants in the La Prairie project. To graduate student Maged Senbel and co-op student Doug Raphael, who assisted me in translating the La Prairie project into a paper the following year and who contributed to the chapter "Planning for Change of New Communities" (Chapter 5).

To architects Robert White and John Archer and graduate students Michael Chan, Jasmin S. Fréchette, Isah Chun Lui, Sigrun Prahl, John-Phillip Reuer, Jennifer E. Steffel, and Yu Wei, who participated in the Notre-Dame-de-Grâce experiment. With Jennifer E. Steffel and Jasmin S. Fréchette I co-authored the paper that later became the thrust of the chapter "Planning for Change within Existing Communities" (Chapter 4).

To graduate students Wen-Chieh (Richard) Lu, Masayoshi Noguchi, Yangli (Michael) Ou, Wei Ma, and Veronica Zidarich, participants in the Atwater Market experiment.

I have been blessed with good students and I would like to thank them all.

I would like to thank the Société d'habitation du Québec, and particularly urbanist Jacques Trudel, for providing financial support to complete the outcome of the La Prairie and Notre-Dame-de-Grâce experiments.

I would like to acknowledge others who have contributed to the creation of this book: student Nadia Meratla, who assembled the first draft and helped transcribe the Atwater Market project; co-op student Richard Boro, who tracked archival material; Peter Reed, who provided planning research; students Michelle Kwok, Karen Hui, and Jing Zhao, who contributed drafting skills; students Carmen Lee and Rem Garavito, who did computer drafting.

I am grateful to John Watt, who helped shape the various components of the manuscript into a cohesive text. To my assistant, David Krawitz, who over the past years has edited the many papers and draft versions that later became the manuscript. His organizational skills were instrumental in creating this book and his devotion to the project has been admirable.

To Professor David Gordon of Queen's University School of Urban and Regional Planning for his invaluable comments on planning issues, editorial suggestions, and critiques, and for contributing information to the chapter "Reformers and Regulations" (Chapter 1).

Finally, to my wife Sorel and children Paloma and Ben for their support and encouragement.

Avi Friedman
Montreal

PLANNING THE NEW SUBURBIA

Flexibility by Design

The planning methods that have created the North American suburb are the end result of an ideological evolution whose beginnings can be traced to the overpopulated and inhospitable cities of the North American and European Industrial Revolution. In the late eighteenth century, urban areas experienced an unprecedented influx of people as a result of the mechanization of industry and subsequent changes in social and economic form. On the North American continent, many urban centres experienced an almost tenfold population increase in the span of only forty years. At that time, however, cities were incapable of handling such drastic changes. The well-documented squalor and disease of the time attest to this incapacity.

Also, as a result, a new breed of social reformers was born whose primary concern was the sensible and commodious design of an urban environment for the new mega-populations of industrial cities. Planners evoked themes of efficiency, morality, and scientific rationalization in trying to balance social welfare and rapid urban growth. Initially, they concerned themselves with the distribution of amenities in relation to new social structure. It became evident, though, that stronger controls were necessary to ensure harmonious and equitable urban existence.

The concepts and controls that these reformers generated and explored have been appropriated, adapted, and applied over time in the interests of designing urban outgrowth (i.e., suburbia). Therefore, a brief consideration of who these design reformers were and the control mechanisms they formulated is vital to understanding the complexities and problems with the modern suburban planning methodology.

Two of the earliest reformers were Robert Owen and Charles Fourier, of England and France, respectively. In an attempt to alleviate the misery of the urban dweller, both

Figure 1.1. Owen's proposed model town is typical of the ideologies of the time. A rigid geometry, consolidated housing, and centralized, enclosed amenities are characteristics that many new social models hoped would provide equitable living conditions (Podmore 1906).

envisioned an ideal city form that would remove the working class from the existing cluttered cities to new developments, structured around a single industry and agriculture.

Owen's city, proposed in 1816, was New Lanark, where, in a repeatable square module, as seen in Figure 1.1, approximately 1,200 people could reside. Housing enclosed a common space. Communal and recreational buildings were located in the public square, while allotment gardens were behind the houses. Though industry was pushed to the periphery of such a development, it should be noted that Owen was a leading industrialist in England, and he therefore provided for a close living relationship to industry and for the retention of industry by private interests. In fact, Owen's model town could be considered a benevolent dictatorship, as he specified not only the town form but also the hygienic and virtuous manner in which inhabitants should live (Cherry 1970; Podmore 1906).

Fourier created a socialist version of roughly the same type of development. Influenced by the French Revolution and desiring to remove the unemployed from the harsh city environment, he proposed the relocation of society into "phalanxes." These were single buildings that could house up to 1,600 people in private apartments. Figure 1.2 shows the design of Fourier's original proposal. Each phalanstery had centralized communal amenities and was situated on a plot of approximately 5,000 acres of land that residents were expected to cultivate, thereby ensuring self-sustenance. Though the socialist foundation of such a design was never realized, the palatial treatment of the architecture was realized at Guise, France. This phalanstery was intended to accommodate workers at an iron foundry owned by Jean-Baptiste Godin (Beecher 1986; Fourier 1971).

A model town that never made it beyond the literary phase of development but which proved to be strongly influential in later practice was put forth by James Silk Buckingham, in England. His book *National Evils and Practical Remedies, with the Plan of a Model Town* was published in 1849. In it he planned both the social and urban form for a model town, which he called Victoria, such that "inhabited by a well organized community ... would banish nearly all the evils of disease, vice, crime, poverty, misery and hostile and antagonistic feelings, from amongst its members." Buckingham specified that there would be no intoxicants, weapons of war, or tobacco in such a town. There would be free education to

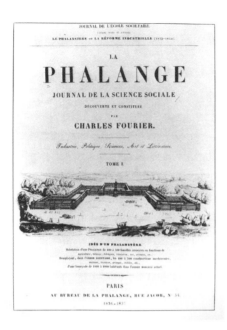

Figure 1.2. In Fourier's design, housing for workers is treated monumentally. In a single building there were apartments for 1,600. From Vol. I (1836) of *La Phalange: Journal de la Science Sociale* (Beecher 1986).

Figure 1.3. Buckingham's theories were of great importance to urban reformers and designers at the end of the nineteenth century. Ebenezer Howard was particularly influenced by Buckingham's book and the design of Victoria (Buckingham 1849).

the age of fifteen, and free health care. The town of Victoria was arranged as a series of concentric squares occupying a square mile of land, with eight main radial roads. The schematic layout of Buckingham's proposal is shown in Figure 1.3. Buckingham went a step further than his predecessors, Owen and Fourier, in that he specified that his town be occupied not by a population related to one industry but for "the great mass of mankind." Victoria had housing and amenities planned to sustain a population of 10,000 (Buckingham 1849; Cherry 1970; Turner 1934).

Two movements that occurred almost simultaneously at the end of the nineteenth century and that have left an indelible mark upon the face of North American planning form (both urban and suburban) were the City Beautiful movement and Ebenezer Howard's Garden City movement.

The City Beautiful movement began at the end of the nineteenth century in the United States. It was referred to at the time as the "American Renaissance," as the country's newly rich considered themselves to be neo-merchant princes and aristocratic patrons of the arts (Kostof 1995). Architecture at this time (such as the Boston Public Library by McKim, Mead, and White) was rich, decadent even, in a way that had not been seen before and perhaps not since in North America. The

Chicago World's Fair of 1893 is credited with stimulating a surge of concern for urban design, which resulted in the spread of the City Beautiful movement (Hodge 1998). Daniel Burnham, the movement's unofficial leader (and designer of Chicago's "White City"), summed up the theory that guided the movement with his famous phrase, "make no little plans for they have no power to stir men's blood." The chief principles were coherence, visual variety, and civic grandeur (Van Nus 1984). This planning movement was intended not only to alter the physical face of the city but to be an urban reform movement that strove to promote health, morality, and equity (Kalman 1994).

Planners who subscribed to the City Beautiful philosophy of classical beaux arts expression and civic grandeur believed that overall planning and uniformity would bring order to urban America. They designed "symmetrically grouped civic centres with malls and administrative and cultural buildings of a uniform classical design" (Kostof 1995). The classical design was typically Greek revival in the United States and Greek and Gothic revival in Canada. In spite of some grand buildings and a new geometry in the city's urban core, the problems of the city raged on. The issues of sufficient housing and public health in the North American city had still not been properly addressed. Though prominent (this planning has left its imprint on cities in the United States such as Chicago and Washington, DC), the City Beautiful movement was an imposed solution to problems that were never really accounted for by this planning. It was a strange response to the problems of a country whose founding premise was democracy.

Social concern was one of the major roots of the City Beautiful movement in Canada. There were great discrepancies between social classes at the time of the movement's beginning: the well-off were powerful and wealthy, while the poor were numerous and lived under extremely trying circumstances, rife with disease and substandard housing. To beautify the city was seen as socially beneficial, because there was a belief that an ugly environment caused psychological damage. The "ugliness" of Canadian cities at the turn of the century was one of the main stimuli for the City Beautiful movement in Canada (Van Nus 1984).

In Canada, the influence of the movement was broadly spread but not widely realized; there were many proposals but few adoptions of complete plans. The grandest proposed plan was in 1914 in Calgary by English landscape architect Thomas H. Mawson (Figure 1.4). He anticipated the planning principle of road hierarchy, but the plan was too ambitious for the time and place. Though a few of the plan's elements were built, the plan was not executed (Kalman 1994). One of Mawson's few Canadian designs to be implemented was that of Saskatchewan's Wascana Centre. Even when Canadian City Beautiful plans were carried out, their main areas of achievement were limited to civic centres, as in Mawson's plans for Regina (Brennan 1994). On a smaller scale, the town of

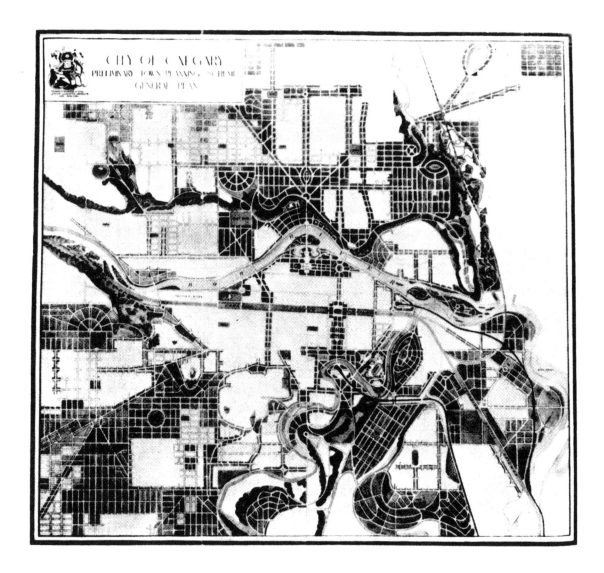

Figure 1.4. The plan of Calgary is typical of the City Beautiful ideal. Radiating diagonals and highly geometric street layouts that led to grand vistas and strong architectural promenades were made popular by such planning (Mawson and Sons 1912).

Maisonneuve, Quebec, was somewhat successful with the creation of a series of public buildings (Kalman 1994). At the turn of the last century, Maisonneuve was termed "the Pittsburgh of Canada," with a growing population and expanding industry. A liberal ideology (belief in progress), prevalent prosperity (which elicited a "general climate of euphoria"), and the new generation of local bourgeoisie (who wanted to "show off its achievements") all contributed to the adoption of City Beautiful plans in Maisonneuve (Linteau 1985). In the end, the Canadian City Beautiful never truly existed and was more of an unattainable ideal. Historically, economically, and socially, it emerged into volatile spheres with optimism and hopes for progress. Administratively, however, it ushered in the birth of planning as a profession.

In 1898, the British planner Ebenezer Howard published a book entitled *Tomorrow: A Peaceful Path to Real Reform* (republished in 1902 as *Garden Cities of Tomorrow*). In it he proposed the withdrawal from already-industrialized cities to communities that combined the social and public conveniences of towns with the healthy and serene aspects of rural life. Howard felt that since private ownership of land led to an exploitation of the city centre and inflation of property values, a community whose land was owned by a limited-dividend company (rid of private speculation) would allow for free buildings, services, and economy. With buildings spread out in a small community setting (Howard initially proposed a 30,000-resident limit), the countryside and its benefits would be accessible to

all. The proposal Howard made for a garden city was diagrammatic (the overall plan is shown in Figure 1.5 on the top with a detail on the bottom), a layered circle (in much the same way that Buckingham designed Victoria as a layered square), and did not specify architectural style. It was circular with industry located at the town centre and surrounded by a ring of parkland. Around the park was a "crystal palace," which was primarily a glass arcade to house a shopping area. The next ring layers were to be houses with attached gardens. These were enclosed by a Grand Avenue 127 m (420 ft) wide, which served to separate the residential from the industrial areas. At the periphery there were rail lines and larger farms (Howard 1902; Macfadyen 1933).

The first implementation of Howard's Garden City concepts can be found in the town of Letchworth, England. In 1903, the Garden City Pioneer Company bought 1,529 hectares (3,822 acres) of land north of London and hired Raymond Unwin and Barry Parker to translate Howard's diagram for the site. Unwin had worked previously in community planning and was involved in the design of New Earswick, a forerunner of sorts to Letchworth, where he developed concepts of low-density housing into a prototype for community design. With Letchworth, the effect was momentous, since he could translate Howard's "mechanistic diagrams into an enduring framework" (Miller 1992). There is a centralized civic area in Letchworth enclosed by a park, and housing that radiates from this centre. Unfortunately, it initially and ultimately lacked the geometrical

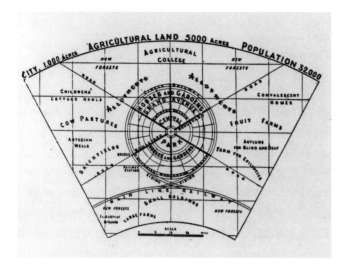

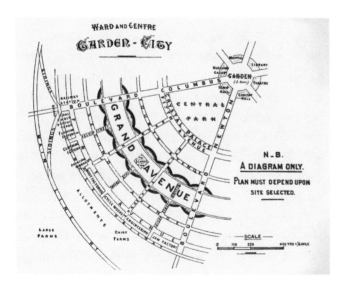

Figure 1.5. Howard's layered design for a garden city is shown on top. In its rigid geometry and somewhat diagrammatic nature, it is possible to see cues taken from Buckingham's Victoria (Howard 1902).

clarity of Howard's planning, and certain features of the town are skewed. For instance, the community could not sustain the public buildings planned for the centre of town; that has left the community, the plan of which is shown in Figure 1.6, somewhat unfocused. In addition, the agricultural ventures were unsuccessful (Unwin 1909; Macfadyen 1933). Letchworth's citizens have complained of the lack of social amenities and the need to travel to London to find them; as well, some of the architectural harmony has been sacrificed with the introduction of garages (F. Jackson 1985). Nonetheless, the economic principles that Howard proposed remain intact: land has remained in common ownership, in spite of private demand to purchase land in the community (Miller 1989). The Letchworth Garden City Heritage Foundation owns and manages a 2,040-hectare (5,100-acre) estate in Letchworth worth 83 million pounds; income generated from the property is used to maintain, improve, and develop the estate and to support its charitable activities (Letchworth Garden City Heritage Foundation 2001).

Before the Second World War, only one more Garden City, Welwyn, was built. The Garden Suburb, a variant of Howard's concept where the development site was the urban edge, turned out to be a more replicable idea. Forest Hill Gardens in Queens, New York, designed by the Olmsted Brothers and Grosvenor Atterbury in 1911, had the sociologist Clarence Perry as a resident; Perry adopted many of its features as elements in his neighbourhood unit (Perry 1929). In the years

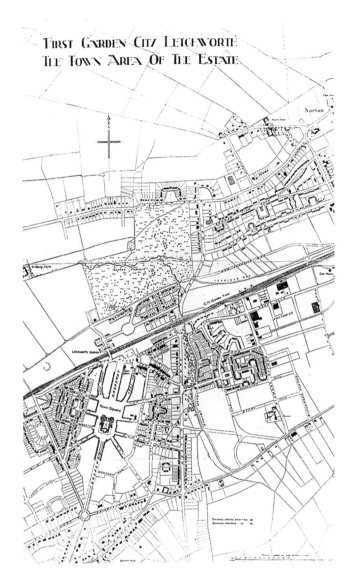

FIRST GARDEN CITY LETCHWORTH
THE TOWN AREA OF THE ESTATE

Figure 1.6. It is possible to see from the plan that Letchworth, though a successful community to this day, lacks the clarity and focus of Howard's theoretical proposal. Letchworth is considered a landmark design in the history of urban planning (Macfadyen 1933).

before the war, there were great opportunities to transform the planning theory that had been developed for the North American continent into real towns. A small group of planners, architects, and historians known as the Regional Planning Association (RPA) became prominent in the planning and execution of these new towns. The RPA lasted from 1923 to 1933 and met two to three times a week, acting as a think tank, a forum for the exchange of ideas. Led by Clarence Stein and Henry Wright, and including Lewis Mumford, the group was very diverse and incorporated the sociology of Charles Horton Cooley and Perry, the civic ideas of Patrick Geddes and Howard, and the educational philosophy of John Dewey. Their goal was to design more humane environments, primarily by acknowledging the Garden City's sensitivities. They aimed to build "balanced communities, cut to the human scale, in balanced regions," continuing to the scale of global balance (Stein 1957). They produced some of America's most progressively planned communities at this time, and remained influential thinkers and writers in the years that followed.

Radburn, New Jersey, is the most renowned product of the Stein-Wright partnership. It is essentially a realistic translation of several of the principles espoused by Howard and put into practice by Unwin and Parker (although houses were sold in Radburn as opposed to being leased in Garden Cities and New Towns in the United Kingdom). Though elements were sacrificed in this implementation (for example, the greenbelt surrounding the town was never purchased because of financial difficulties, and the proposed industrial areas were abandoned due to the Depression), the overall result was a safe, healthy community for young families. There was a variety of housing types in Radburn, and neighbourhoods were serviced by small retail centres and defined by cul-de-sacs and scenic, curving streets. Part of Radburn's success was with its accommodation of the automobile, whereby the pedestrian and the automobile were completely separated (Parsons 1992). This new phenomenon stimulated many novel development patterns. Housing was arranged in large blocks with interior greens; the innovative use of the cul-de-sac created these "superblocks," each one 14 to 20 hectares (35 to 50 acres) in size (Lynch 1981). There were specialized circulation patterns to separate pedestrian and vehicular traffic via interior paths and overpasses. Although most dwellings in Radburn were single-family, there were some rental units in garden apartments (Schoenauer 2000). Individual unit planning was oriented towards the internal open areas rather than to the streets. These design articulations, as can be read from the community plan in Figure 1.7, made Radburn a model of planning in suburbia for the next thirty years.

A development that looked to Radburn, at least superficially, as a model and in whose likeness most of the late twentieth century's suburbs have been built was Levittown, Pennsylvania (Figure 1.8). Laid out by a private concern on a flat site, the town was designed for a homogeneous population—the young, white, middle-class, car-dependent,

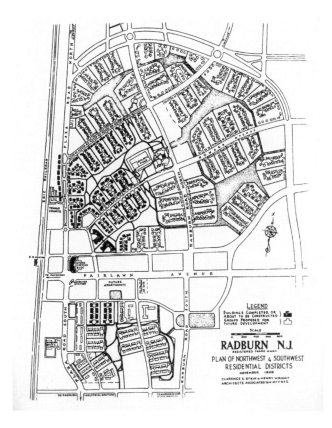

Figure 1.7. Though not a direct translation of Howard's Garden City proposal, Radburn is considered important because of its picturesque treatment of the New Jersey countryside and its acknowledgment of the growing importance of the automobile in twentieth-century living (Radburn Association 1929).

mom-dad-and-the-kids family. It lacked the Garden City's ideological roots (there is no separation of pedestrian and vehicular traffic and the curving streets are arbitrary as there is very little topography to respond to). Also, there was no localized industry or business—it was intended to house those workers commuting to Philadelphia or to the Fairless

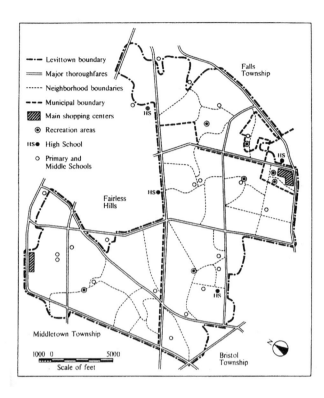

Figure 1.8. In the plan of Levittown, Pennsylvania, it is important to note the total lack of local commerce or industry. Levittown is, perhaps, the prototypical bedroom community (Popenoe 1977).

Works of United States Steel, which was nearby. The 17,300 houses that eventually comprised Levittown were poorly insulated, had no solar orientation, and were spread over 2,300 hectares (5,750 acres) on 1,300 streets (Gans 1967; Van der Ryn and Calthorpe 1986). Though the town was a capital exercise in inefficiency, the Levittown Company profited handsomely from the development. Nearly unlimited,

cheap land resources and standardization made such towns popular with developers throughout the North American continent.

It is interesting to note that throughout the history of new planning there run broad, common themes (for instance, the separation of residential and industrial areas). It is easy to believe that as these common themes became understood, controls intended to regulate them developed. Running parallel to the historical evolution of suburban built form, therefore, is the development of methods of regulation and implementation of this form. In his seminal work, *An Introduction to City Planning*, Benjamin C. Marsh noted in 1909 that "the most important part of city planning ... is the districting of the city into zones or districts." It is this "districting," its development, and its modern form that will be considered in the remainder of this chapter.

The first zoning regulations in North America attempted to limit the spread of commercial and industrial areas into residential neighbourhoods. The Consolidated Municipal Act of 1904, for example, gave the right to control the "location, erection and use of buildings for laundries, butcher shops, stores and manufacturers" to cities in the province of Ontario, Canada (Rogers 1973). Through height limitations and minimum setback requirements within sections of the city, early zoning rules contributed substantially to determining the character of neighbourhoods. The most far-reaching zoning control, and the continent's first comprehensive zoning law at the beginning of the twentieth century, was drafted in 1916 by the Heights of Buildings Commission of New York City. An appeal to the residents of New York City drafted by the commission is shown in Figure 1.9. Reform activists joined members of the commission, most of whom were real estate investors, in the interests of saving their city from the detrimental impact of the Manhattan skyscraper.

While reformers sought the preservation of light and fresh air at street level, investors who owned property in the city centre wanted to stop the rush-hour chaos created by the great number of workers from office buildings and immigrant labourers from factories that had relocated to the area. Although legitimized by the reformers' arguments, this legislation was far from altruistic. From the beginning, land-use regulations subordinated the interests of health and safety to those of property values. The 1913 report published by the commission noted that "restriction should be framed with a view to securing to each district as much light, air, relief from congestion, and safety from fire as is consistent with a proper regard for the most beneficial use of the land and as is practicable under existing conditions as to improvements and land values" (Toll 1969).

Eventually, the commission realized that regulating building height was only a partial solution to the city's problems. Citywide zoning was the answer. The ruling of *Brown v. Maryland*

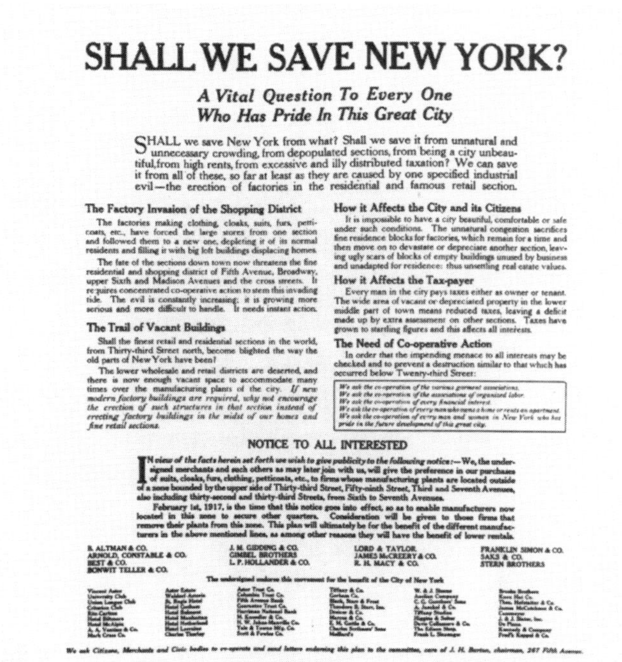

Figure 1.9. In 1917, the Heights of Buildings Commission of New York City made an impassioned (and, in hindsight, ultimately futile) plea to the residents of the city. It is widely held that this original commission was, to a great extent, the creation of a few wealthy real estate developers (Burton 1916).

by the United States Supreme Court was the first ruling of this kind, which assured that "the states had the inherent power and the reserved power to pass laws for the health, safety, order and general welfare of their communities" (Toll 1969). This "general welfare" stipulation as justification for zoning still stands today.

On 25 July 1916, comprehensive zoning became law in New York City. Shortly thereafter, metropolitan areas across the

United States, realizing zoning's vast potential for changing the faces of crowded industrial areas, followed suit with their own zoning laws. Though zoning mandates come from state or provincial legislatures, the immense demand for zoning powers spurred the federal Advisory Commission on Zoning, as created by US Secretary of Commerce Herbert Hoover, to issue the Standard State Enabling Act in 1924. This was boiler-plate legislation that state governments could pass verbatim to quickly give municipal governments the power to zone (Toll 1969).

Zoning attracted diverse supporters: real estate developers, who saw in it stabilized property values and security in lending; public administrators, who recognized it as a cost-saving mechanism in the provision of public services; mayors, who saw it as the key to containing blight and preserving the city's tax base; reformers and designers, who sought loftier, deterministic design goals; and homeowners, who desired the simple assurance of neighbourhood stability (Haar 1989). For all these reasons, zoning was regarded as essential to the success of America's communities. In 1916, only eight cities in the United States had zoning controls. By 1920, the number had jumped to eighty-two, with a total of 904 zoning ordinances in existence (Feagin 1989).

Canadian planners keenly observed these events occurring in the United States and pushed to make comprehensive zoning a component of their urban vocabulary. Though it was common practice of American municipalities to enact zoning legislation without the presence of any city plan, Canadian planners emulated their British counterparts in the consistent use of comprehensive planning. Consequently, in the majority of Canadian provinces the adoption of land-use bylaws must conform to the basis of a plan (Rogers 1973).

The first comprehensive Canadian zoning bylaw was enacted in 1924 for Kitchener, Ontario, by planners Thomas Adams and Horace Seymour. Restrictions on land use had existed for quite some time before this, however. Efforts were made to separate residential from non-residential areas within cities, as with a 1904 bylaw enacted in Toronto. Also in 1904, cities in Ontario had the right to control the location, erection, and use of buildings for "laundries, butcher shops, stores, and manufactories" (Hodge 1998). These piecemeal approaches were criticized by planners as being unequal and ineffective in comprehensively planning a city.

Thomas Adams was very influential in creating zoning legislation in Canada. In 1914, the Canadian Commission of Conservation hired him as a town planning consultant to the federal government. He visited most of the Canadian provinces and lobbied for and wrote planning legislation for many of them. During the first decades of the century, planning legislation was prepared for most of the provinces, though these planning acts were "tame by today's standards"; planning and zoning existed, but planning was limited to the urban fringe and not for "replanning existing areas" (Wolfe 1994). Planning in Canada was not without its detractors. Though Adams stressed that urban planning was a "business proposition"—its primary preoccupations being convenience, economy, and easy transport—"town planning broke upon the Canadian people as an expensive decorative luxury" (Simpson 1985).

By definition, zoning is merely a planning tool. Its classifications allocate portions of land into defined character groups based upon the organizational concept of the comprehensive plan. The major subject areas, which are prescribed by zoning, are the use of land (residential, commercial, or industrial), population density, building bulk, off-street parking, and smaller issues, such as view protection. The designated areas are recorded on a zoning map, an example of which is shown in Figure 1.10, which is intended to be essentially self-administering.

Zoning ordinances are customarily based on predetermined compatibility of various land uses. This can easily produce functionally inefficient land-use patterns. For example, cumulative or pyramid zoning, which has been in use since planning's earliest days, positions a narrowly defined residential classification at the top of its zoning scale and an open classification at the bottom. As classification type moves from the top of the scale to the bottom, the number of permitted uses at each successive level increases. This sort of scheme prevents anticipation of

infrastructure and service demands, and often results in wastefully organized resources (Roeseler and McClendon 1986).

In theory, the presence of a comprehensive plan indicates that the municipality has taken into consideration the needs of its entire community. Subsequent zoning ordinances passed in accordance with the plan, it follows, should be in the interest of the general welfare. Conversely, zoning ordinances passed without the control of a well-designed and equitable comprehensive plan (or in the absence of any plan at all) are at best arbitrary and likely to be inefficient. At worst, they may be exclusionary.

When planning was in its infancy and the concept of the comprehensive plan had not yet been developed, zoning ordinances were most likely to respond to pressures to stabilize or bolster property values. At that time, "the greatest concern which planners could expect to gain over the efficiency of urban development was that of coordinator of the various economic interests which affected development" (Van Nus 1979). One of the immediate repercussions of early zoners' uninformed and unstructured decision making was overzoning. Zoning became an instrument of aggressive speculation as property owners exerted political pressure in the interests of having land zoned for maximum use. Unknowing politicians permitted such zoning decisions because they raised the community tax base. In many instances, the results were outrageous: in Los Angeles there was enough land zoned for

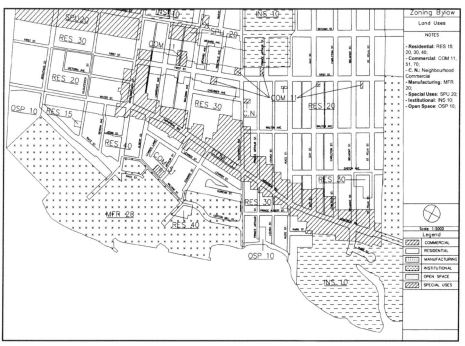

ZONE	DESCRIPTION	PERMITTED USES
RES 15	Residential	Single-family dwelling, rooming or boarding house, duplex, semi-detached dwelling, home occupation, office of physician or dentist, school, church, hospital, community centre, incidental accessory building
RES 20	Residential	RES 15 + triplex, quadruplex, rowhouse
RES 30	Residential	RES 20 + walk-up apartment buildings
RES 40	Residential	Existing single- and two-family dwellings, rooming or boarding house, multi-family dwelling, home occupation, office of physician or dentist, school, church, hospital, community centre, private club, service commercial uses within multiple-family dwelling, incidental accessory building
COM 11	Commercial	Business or professional office, government building, institutional building, service shop, self-service laundry, retail shop, funeral home, printing establishment, hotel, restaurant, motel, food supermarket, service station, place of recreational assembly, parking lot, storage garage, accessory buildings
COM70	Commercial	COM 11 + dwelling units on second floor, commercial school
MFR 20	Manufacturing	Machine shop, service station, food locker, building materials yard, laundry and cleaners, contractor equipment, warehouse, retail lumber yard, workshops, feed or fuel yard, transport terminal, laboratories, government yard, animal hospital, used car lot, athletic and health clubs, taxi depot, food preparation, business and professional offices, factory retail, manufacturer, accessory buildings, research and development facility
INS 10	Institutional	Single-family dwelling, rooming or boarding house, duplex, semi-detached dwelling, multiple-family dwelling, home occupation, office of physician or dentist, school, church, hospital, community centre, private club, institutions, clinics, incidental accessory building
OSP 10	Open Space	Public park, playground, playing field, tennis court, bowling green, swimming pool, ice rink, or similar recreational use; community hall, sports arena, library, art gallery, museum, dock, boathouse, marina, single-family dwelling for employees on premises

Figure 1.10. The zoning map of the Le Village district of Cornwall, Ontario, is typical of this control. Easily understood codes for land uses are superimposed on a schematic map of the area in point (Friedman 1999).

business to support the economic activity of the entire American population; the business zoning for Duluth, Minnesota, could have supported a population of 20 million; New York City could have housed 77 million people, while its commercial district's working capacity was 344 million (Toll 1969). This frivolous speculation and distortion of proper land uses contributed greatly to the deterioration of the urban core and acceleration of urban sprawl.

The distortions that were occurring in the city were also occurring in the undeveloped periphery of North America's urban areas. Planners viewed the newly accessible "urban frontier" as a blank canvas, with zoning the equivalent of a paint-by-numbers pattern for settlement. The renowned British planner Thomas Adams, while working in Canada, said that "it was in control of new suburban development that the greatest opportunity lay for successful zoning ... because vested interests in existing buildings had not yet been created" (Van Nus 1979). That may have been so, but indigenous planners were not yet capable of making concise, informed development decisions. They frequently mandated that initial residential or commercial development in a new area be allowed to dictate the course of future development.

From its beginnings, the potential of zoning as a planning tool was exaggerated in order to win support. It was touted as a route to neighbourhood stability, efficient service provision, lower property taxes, and reduced crowding. It was not long before planners realized its limitations: merely to dictate what can and cannot be built. Zoning did not provide a mechanism that could actively guide what was going to be built. "It was not because zoning was getting 'distorted' or 'misused' that the reform-minded planners and city administrators were getting disillusioned with it, but because the true essence of zoning was beginning to assert itself against the naive expectations of these professionals" (Hason 1977).

Essentially, zoning is an instrument, designed specifically to reduce irrationalities or externalities in the market. In order to carry out their primary function as an economic stabilizer, zoning ordinances must be both rigidly consistent and permanent. But because planners operate outside the economic market, there is no negative feedback mechanism for correcting zoning mistakes. Zoning is likely to function as too rigid a control during times of change and, in doing so, institutionalize mistakes.

Whether or not zoning ordinances follow a comprehensive plan, a zoning strategy will have a resounding impact on development, regardless of the motivation of the underlying approach. When combined with a demographic or economic variable, the practice of planning often excludes any possibility of zoning flexibility. The nature of this rigidity is a profound neglect of the dynamic quality of the circumstances in which society exists.

Possibilities to modify zoning do exist. These include the appeal of decisions made by building officials, getting variances to prevent "unnecessary hardship" due to "unique circumstances," establishing special exceptions such as "conditional

TYPE	DESCRIPTION	APPLICATION	ENFORCEMENT
Land Subdivision Control	• Regulate development of vacant or undeveloped areas • Create high-quality physical environment • Ensure voicing of concerns of interested parties	Applied to new developments	Enforced by municipality
Building Code	• Protection of public health, safety, and property • Establishment of minimum construction standards	Universally applied in a jurisdiction (town, city, province)	Enforced by local building departments
Zoning Ordinances	• Regulate land usage and building construction • Ensure public access to light, air, and open space • Protection and stability of property values • Protection against aesthetic nuisances	Applied over an entire municipality (not site-specific)	Enforced by city, town, or village municipalities
Deed Restrictions	• Regulate land usage and building construction • Regulate visual environment and building form • Protection and stability of property values • Protection against aesthetic nuisances	Applied on an individual lot basis	Privately imposed by developer/neighbourhood association
Design Review	• Monitor the overall design process • Advise and approve architectural design based on the judgment of individual board members	Applied on an individual lot basis	Enforced by authority of a review board
Design Guidelines	• Establishment of minimum construction standards • Regulate land usage and building construction • Protection and stability of property values • Protection against aesthetic nuisances • Regulate visual environment and building form	Not necessarily applied to a specific site (can be theoretical and generically based)	Not enforceable or legally binding

Figure 1.11. There are various methods of controlling development besides zoning. The most common controls are shown in point form here (after Dent 1993).

uses" or "special use permits," and rarely making amendments (National Commission 1973). This raises the question: if such changes are permissible on an ad hoc basis, what specific economic protection does zoning provide? The answer is that though zoning is a major form of development control in North America, other control mechanisms are necessary to regulate development to an acceptable degree. Mechanisms that act in conjunction with zoning are summarized in Figure 1.11.

Land subdivision control is a land-use planning tool used to regulate the development of vacant or undeveloped areas, especially new developments on the edges of cities. It gives municipalities—often together with the province or state—the authority to approve land subdivision plans and ensure that they meet local standards of health, safety, and convenience. Subdivision control has two main components: it attempts to create high-quality physical environments, and it operates as a monitoring process to ensure the voicing of concerns of interested parties (Hodge 1998). In suburban development, land subdivision control can be the key planning tool, with residential zoning following as a result of subdivision approval.

Similar to zoning codes, building codes are established through a municipal ordinance. A building code is a set of government regulations that impose minimum construction, structural, and mechanical standards on building in order to protect public health and safety. Given that building codes regulate some aspects of a building's design and most aspects of construction, alteration, material use, and occupancy, their impact on urban form should not be underestimated.

There is a hierarchical ladder of codes, each code having its own scale and emphasis. Governments commonly compile

DESCRIPTION OF MEMBRANE	FIRE-RESISTANCE RATING, MIN
15.9 mm Type X gypsum wallboard with ≥75 mm mineral wool batt insulation above wallboard	30
19 mm gypsum-sand plaster on metal lath	30
Double 14.0 mm Douglas-fir plywood phenolic bonded	30
Double 12.7 mm Type X gypsum wallboard	45
25 mm gypsum-sand plaster on metal lath	45
Double 15.9 mm Type X gypsum wallboard	60
32 mm gypsum-sand plaster on metal lath	60

Figure 1.12. A table from the National Building Code of Canada: Table D-2.3.12. Fire-Resistance Rating for Ceiling Membranes (National Research Council 1995).

WALLS	TRIM AND SASH	SHUTTERS OR DOORS	DOORS	CHIMNEYS	FLY SCREENS	ROOF
White	White	Dark green	White	Brick painted white	White	Dark green
Silver grey	White	Bottle green	White	Red sand-moulded brick	White	Weathered grey
Ivory	Ivory	Olive green	Ivory	Red sand-moulded brick	Ivory	Dark moss green
Shingles stained to weather to natural wood tone	White	Blue green	Ivory	Common brick sand face, light range of red, brown, and salmon	Ivory	Very dark grey

Figure 1.13. A deed restriction for houses in Shaker Heights. The colour palate and materials used can be dictated by such controls (Shaker Village Standards 1928).

a national building code (the US has four "Model Codes" that correspond to the four regions of the country, and Canada has one national building code), which covers generalized aspects of building that apply to construction over a vast area. In Figure 1.12, a table from the 1995 National Building Code of Canada is shown. Municipalities are not required to adopt the national-level codes in their entirety. These are often supplemented by provincial or state codes that define regulations referring to the particular climatic, geographical, and cultural concerns of that province or state. Companion codes are often instituted to govern specific aspects of building, such as energy conservation or accessibility to handicapped persons. Having scaled codes allows municipalities to account for differences in regional traditions and preferences, though it may also interfere with design and the efficient distribution of materials, as architects and contractors must be familiar with the intricacies of the codes that apply to a particular region. Also, social and demographic changes are often unacknowledged in building codes because of the irregular frequency and layered bureaucracy associated with the upgrade process. Because of the legality of their implementation, building codes, along with zoning, are the least flexible of control mechanisms in planning today.

Deed restriction is a form of privately administered developmental regulation. It is an agreement in a deed of sale that legally binds the holder to certain requirements or provisions that may restrict future use or modification of the land by the

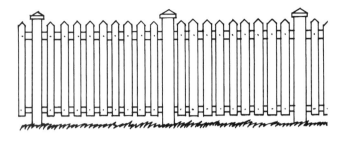

Figure 1.14. The City of Westmount in Quebec has restrictions on the appearance of external property characteristics, drafted by the members of the design review board. The above example is a sample of the design restrictions on fencing post tops (Westmount Architectural and Planning Commission 1987).

buyer. Such restrictions can be significantly far-reaching, regulating broad issues like site coverage, density, and use of all buildings on the site. Deed restrictions can also address small issues such as materials used and architectural style. One section of the deed restriction for houses in Shaker Heights, Ohio, regarding a colour palate and material use is illustrated in Figure 1.13. Legislators can no longer, however, institute restrictions that are in violation of civil rights legislation. The contractual agreement lasts over a period of time, ranging from ten to one hundred years. Deed restrictions are one of the few forms of architectural controls that acknowledge the passage of time and the possibility of transformations occurring in a given period. Though the longevity of deed restrictions often maintains old-fashioned or obsolete developmental conditions, a certain degree of flexibility is achieved because of the limited duration of the restriction. After the restrictions have expired, the situation can be assessed and the agreement conditions reviewed or discarded.

Design review is a method of monitoring the overall design process by requiring board approval for new construction. Review can occur at various levels—neighbourhood, municipal, or state—and can address issues such as historical authenticity and environmental impact, though the scope of the review is typically restricted to the external appearance of the proposed structure, such as the example in Figure 1.14. Members of a design review board are either elected or appointed for varying lengths of time, depending on the board's constitution, and should come from a variety of backgrounds, representative of a cross-section of the residents of their jurisdiction. The design review board operates as an adjunct to other methods of developmental regulation. Its findings are not legally binding, though they are enforceable in conjunction with zoning ordinances or homeowners association contracts.

As a final example of historically significant urban planning, the work of Andres Duany and Elizabeth Plater-Zyberk at Seaside, Florida, should be considered to illustrate how well typical control mechanisms can work when they are creatively augmented to accommodate a new social picture.

Flexibility at the scale of the individual building is the primary focus of the planning and controls at Seaside. Seaside is a large residential community that follows a comprehensive master plan. This is a fairly conventional practice. It is innovative, however, in its control over the final execution of building design. Contrary to accepted planning methodology, Duany and Plater-Zyberk (proponents of the New Urbanism) view statistic-based planning as one of the main sources of blight in most of post-Second World War development. Consequently, their strategy revisits the turn-of-the-century concepts of civic form, as derived from the beaux arts principles of classical composition. They have attempted to recreate the kind of community that flourished in America from the end of the nineteenth century until the beginning of the Second World War. The two travelled from Key West to New Orleans studying Southern small-town forms as precedents. The towns on which Seaside was based were orderly settlements with classical relationships of well-proportioned buildings flanking central axes and terminating in well-identifiable landmarks (Abrams 1986; Duany et al. 2000; Easterling 1985; Duany and Plater-Zyberk 1991; Mohney and Easterling 1991).

Duany and Plater-Zyberk were commissioned to design a resort town on a 32-hectare (80-acre) plot of land inherited by developer Robert Davis on Florida's Gulf Coast Panhandle. In their experiment, the awareness of the automobile (a dynamic that did not enter into the formation of precedent examples) was acute. They maintained that the automobile need not be excluded from a healthy, vigorous development—this modern reliance could be accommodated, they hypothesized. Also, the palate of architectural design was sensitively treated in order to create the desired richness and animated character of a small town, anchored in successful examples of the local vernacular types. And rather than design the entire community, they restricted their involvement to the creation of an urban code that handled all development in the area, with regard to uniform stylistic expression and harmonious form. They allowed for variety and diversity in the individual realization of a prescribed code. In 1983, after five years of research and development, the town master plan, as seen in Figure 1.15, was unveiled. It proposed 350 dwellings, 100 to 200 lodging units, a retail centre downtown, and a conference hall for civic presence.

Individual sections within the overall master plan are zoned by type of architectural style rather than by the traditional zoning of functional type. Aside from the communal and public buildings that follow a consistent distinguishable typology, the town is divided into eight sections, each with a vernacular architectural style of the southeastern United States. The eight sections also include different occupancies, such as strictly residential, residential and lodging, residential and retail, or residential and light industrial. Each use and style is intended to create a distinct and cohesive neighbourhood. Together, the eight districts should create a diversified and architecturally rich town.

Duany and Plater-Zyberk's urban design code has a decisive simplicity. The primary control consists of a single table of two-dimensional annotated figures that guide the execution of building type so as to form a harmonious streetscape. There

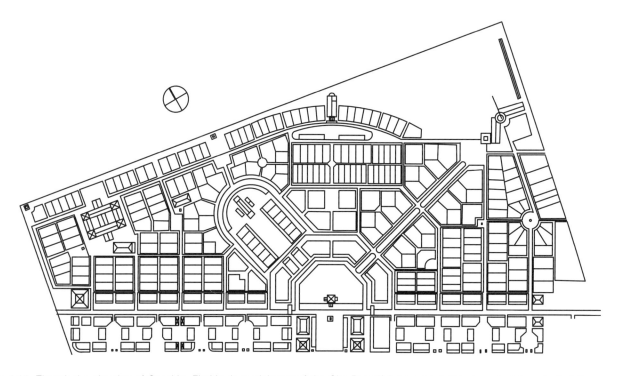

Figure 1.15. Though the planning of Seaside, Florida, is reminiscent of the City Beautiful movement, it is important to note that the grand avenues and geometrical layout were not implemented with a lack of awareness of its inhabitants. In addition, the accommodation of modern idiosyncrasies, such as the automobile, in a traditional, picturesque setting has made Seaside a wildly popular resort development (Duany and Plater-Zyberk 1991).

are other architectural controls at Seaside, which are set in a written and graphic code, illustrated in Figure 1.16. Compulsory rules are established (for instance, the colour of all public buildings must be white, even though the style and design is left open for the developer to decide), and all buildings must pass through a review process before construction begins. Furthermore, every year a different architect is hired to oversee the review process, which ensures a level of variety within the established order.

The town of Seaside has received international acclaim as a model community. Its picturesque and harmonious character

has, in fact, created such fame that there have been adverse effects on the intended social and economic mix of the community. Land prices have soared higher than those of adjacent sites, making it impossible for lower-income families to purchase land or even rent lodging.

The key to Seaside's planning success is the degree to which architectural control and individual freedom of expression have been balanced. Fundamental to the creation of such balance is the simplicity and clarity of the urban code. In it builders have a prescribed mandate to conform within the overall harmony of the community, but at the same time they

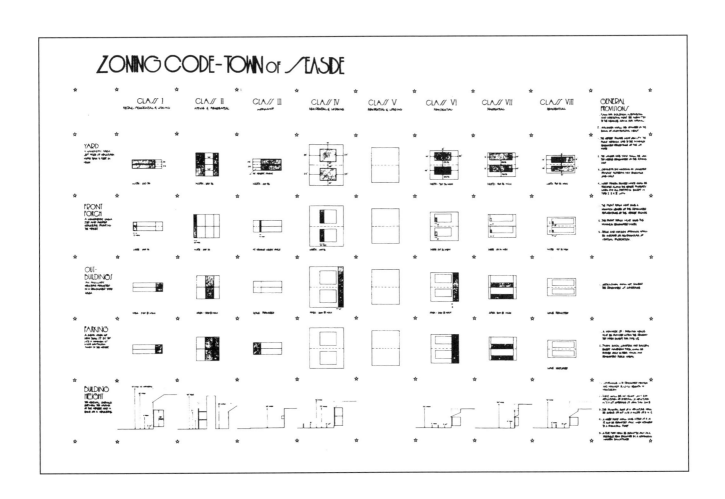

Figure 1.16. A page from the zoning code of Seaside. The variety of multiple-use land-use designations is one of the main reasons this development is considered a lively and healthy one, though, in orthodox planning, multiple usage is typically frowned upon (Duany and Plater-Zyberk 1991).

are afforded freedom of expression within these set boundaries. The resulting flexibility of this pre-planned community is unique, though typical planning controls (occupancy rules, lot divisions, and building-type restrictions) render Seaside's master plan as inflexible, at times, as that of any staid and less meticulously controlled suburb in North America.

In the chapters that follow, a consideration of suburbia (its present state and how it has evolved) shall be made, as well as of precedent models for flexible, healthy outgrowth. This material having been presented, the next step will then be articulated: a reconsideration of planning practices and beliefs as they exist at present. As illustrated in this chapter, planning ideologies and concepts have responded to societal needs; their evolution has been part of the entire process.

2

E v o l u t i o n   o f   t h e
S u b u r b a n
I d e a l

Suburbia arguably dominates the North American housing environment: a higher proportion of North Americans now live in the suburbs than in either rural or urban areas. According to the American Housing Survey, 47% of the total American population lives in suburban areas (US Bureau of the Census 1999). It has been realized that, contrary to its initial intention of being a combination of city and country life, suburbia can claim to be a separate urban form.

It is important, therefore, to understand not only the personalities, theories, and controls that have shaped the modern suburban form but also the numerous stimuli, applied both from governmental and private interests, that have, over time, shaped the residential pattern in which most of North America lives. In understanding these influences, it becomes clear that further evolution of suburban form is required to respond to the constantly changing stresses with which society will be living.

In 1820, only 7% of the American population lived in cities (and of this 7%, the majority resided in either New York or Philadelphia). Only ten cities in the entire country could boast populations greater than 10,000. North America at this time was not an urban continent. This condition did not last. As the Industrial Revolution spread from England to North America, urban populations skyrocketed. By 1860, New York City had over one million residents, and seven other cities had populations that exceeded 100,000. By 1890, New York City was approaching the size of London, while Philadelphia and Chicago were each home to a million residents. One-half of all the people in the northeastern United States had become urban, as had one-third of America's entire population (K. Jackson 1985).

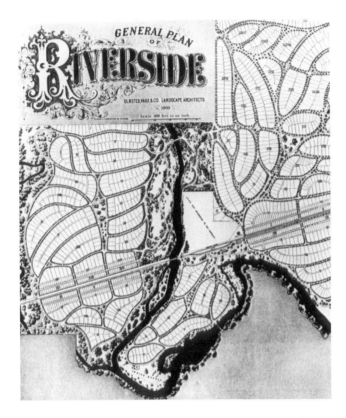

Figure 2.1. Riverside, Illinois, was designed by a prominent landscape architecture firm of the day, Olmsted, Vaux and Company. A clear symbiotic relationship was meant to be established between nature, topography, and these new homes for the wealthy (Olmsted 1992).

areas in order to access cheap immigrant labour and transportation hubs, the resulting noise, dirt, and density greatly damaged the livability of these North American cities. It is no surprise, therefore, that before urban reformers began working to extricate the working masses, exodus from the city was an option only for the rich.

Expensive and limited steam railroad lines provided a means of travel between the city and wealthy enclaves, which were developed at the periphery of city limits. The earliest of these enclaves, such as Llewellyn Park, New Jersey (planned in 1853), and Riverside, Illinois (planned in 1869 and shown in Figure 2.1), were novel residential experiences. Often planned by landscape architects, neighbourhoods had gently curving streets that conformed to natural topography and created idyllic settings. The average lot size in Llewellyn Park, whose infrastructure included wells and septic tanks, was bigger than the lot size in Riverside, which was serviced with gas, water, and sewers. Picturesque homes on large lots (much larger on average than twentieth-century suburban lots) were designed, emphasizing the communities' decidedly non-urban image (MacBurnie 1992). These early suburban homes strove to represent a new domestic ideal. They combined a careful treatment of outdoor spaces with an emphasis on feminine utilitarianism, and evoked images of the European cottage. One of these early suburban homes is shown in Figure 2.2. As retreats, they expressed the nineteenth century female's goal of domesticity. The home replaced nature as a source of

Pre-Industrial Revolution cities had easily definable spatial characteristics. These included very high densities and clearly defined city limits. Also, mixed land uses provided people with the luxury of living close to their workplace; often, the most respectable addresses were at the city's core. With industrialization came a change in the prioritization of urban spaces. When industries moved into the downtown spiritual renewal, and romanticized the benefits of private space. At the same time, these houses reflected the male homeowner's education, affluence, morality, orderliness, and faith in the nation (Marsh 1990). The middle-class family became increasingly nuclear and private as a result of changing gender roles and the new relationship between the home and workplace.

Public opinion gradually replaced the city with the suburb as the ideal place to raise a family. The suburban lifestyle was absorbed by the mainstream North American social and cultural value system. Despite the attraction of this new lifestyle, it took a series of transportation innovations to provide accessibility for the middle class. The horse-drawn omnibus was introduced to New York City in 1829 and the horsecar in 1852. Both of these means of transport accelerated cross-town travel and made it socially acceptable to commute for the general population. The electric streetcar, however, was the key to providing access to the suburbs for the vast majority of the population. First successfully introduced in the United States in 1887, this rapid, inexpensive, and manure-free mode of transportation finally enabled the middle class to move beyond the confines of the city on a daily basis (K. Jackson 1985).

Land speculators, many of whom also owned streetcar companies, dictated the course of early suburban development. Transit tycoons made fortunes by buying land outside the city limits and bringing the street to it. Convenient access to the city

Figure 2.2. The earliest suburbs were retreats for the wealthier members of mid-nineteenth-century society. Houses manifested the new middle-class attitudes regarding public and private space and gendered space, among others, which were forming at the time (Western Horticultural Review 1850).

became a major selling point and assured future development of the site. The foreseeable result of this private speculative development was sprawl.

To ensure a profitable volume of commuters, such streetcar suburbs required a fairly high density. In fact, they initially resembled housing of a more urban type, simply removed from the urban setting. A typical American home along an established transportation corridor sat on a 0.04-hectare lot

Figure 2.3. Suburban houses intended to be affordable to the majority of urban North Americans were built in great number at the beginning of the twentieth century and following the First World War. Though they were comparatively dense and similar in built form to urban housing, they were desirable because of their pretense of being suburban (Wood 1910).

(one-tenth of an acre). Often these early suburbs formed as an extension of the grid pattern of an existing city, and though "the houses stood apart from each other, [they were] in all features identical with that constructed far nearer city centres, [making] the tacit assumption of urbanity" (Stilgoe 1988). An early drawing of these later suburban homes is shown in Figure 2.3. Although these developments differ substantially from the more affluent suburbs, they were an attainable form of the domesticity and household privacy that the middle class now sought.

The First World War drew a great number of war workers to urban areas across North America. The exodus following the war pushed the postwar suburban construction boom to new heights. In the United States, housing starts increased by nearly 10% annually in the 1920s, and by 1930, 48% of American households owned their own homes (Marsh 1990). Also, the car had become a permanent fixture in the middle-class lifestyle. Initially, acceptance of the automobile was

somewhat reserved—it was viewed as a glamorous toy for the well-to-do. This situation did not last, as the car became an affordable mode of private transportation. In 1898, for example, there was only one car per 18,000 people in the United States. The lack of infrastructure and service facilities, as well as the fact that cars frequently scared the horses, which dominated the city streets, inhibited the car's popularity. As the automobile became increasingly convenient, however, the pace of acceptance naturally accelerated. Primarily because of the affordability and tremendous popularity of Henry Ford's Model T, by 1913 the ratio of cars to people in the United States had increased to one in eight. In 1925, Ford's revolutionary factories produced 9,000 cars per day, and by 1927 the United States was home to 26 million cars (K. Jackson 1985). The American government responded with new policies, technology, and taxes to implement a highway system. The new highways quickly became the arteries of American life.

Prior to the devastation of the Great Depression, North American federal governments believed that housing was essentially the responsibility of the free market. Pressure for housing assistance and economic recovery during the crisis of the 1930s compelled governments to reconsider this position. The United States took an aggressive stance towards housing when, in 1933, the Homeowners Loan Corporation (HOLC) was established. Its purpose was to provide refinancing for households that faced foreclosure and to recover properties that had already been defaulted on. Another New Deal program, the

National Housing Act, which created the Federal Housing Administration (FHA) in 1934, guaranteed mortgages, thereby easing the pressure of the immense housing demand. The FHA agreed to insure long-term fully amortized mortgages provided by private lenders. This increased accessibility to housing by reducing the lenders' risk, thereby increasing their willingness to lend while limiting their down payment requirements and interest rates (Marsh 1990). These terms opened homeownership to the working class, and soon the suburban family with a new house and a long-term FHA mortgage became the symbol of the American way. Largely through FHA programs, equity was introduced to the estates of 35 million households between 1933 and 1978 (K. Jackson 1985). The flip side of this institutionalized suburbanization was the loss of middle-class citizens and middle-class stability in urban areas.

The FHA's "conservative" policies strongly favoured single-family over multi-family dwellings, new construction over rehabilitation of existing units, and, perhaps most insidiously, all-white neighbourhoods over racially diverse areas. The FHA "helped to turn the building industry against the minority and inner city housing market, and its policies supported the income and racial segregation of suburbia. For perhaps the first time, the federal government embraced the discriminatory attitudes of the marketplace. Previously, prejudices were personalized and individualized; FHA exhorted segregation and enshrined it as public policy" (K. Jackson 1985).

The continent's all-consuming mobilization during the Second World War diverted materials and labour from housing production. Would-be homebuyers had to put their aspirations on hold. The rampant postwar consumerism coupled with the great number of returning GIs (and the baby boom that followed closely afterwards) created a terrific housing demand. This demand was reinforced by the United States government's "official endorsement and support of the view that sixteen million GIs of World War II should return to civilian life with a home of their own" (K. Jackson 1985). The most conservative of FHA estimates indicated that responding to the demand would immediately require the construction of 5 million new units, and a total of 12.5 million over the following decade (Wright 1981).

In the United States, the Veterans Administration (VA) in 1944 created a mortgage guarantee program as part of the GI Bill of Rights. It bolstered the demand for owner-occupied units by enabling veterans to borrow the entire appraised value of a house (Wright 1981). From the sheer number of houses that were now likely to be built, it was clear that traditional practices of housing development by numerous small-scale builders would be insufficient for the task.

The government responded with assurances and financing programs that would make it profitable for developers to build mass-produced developments on vast tracts of land. For the first time in history, large-scale builders did the majority of construction. By 1949, for example, 70% of the building of new homes in the United States was done by only 10% of the firms

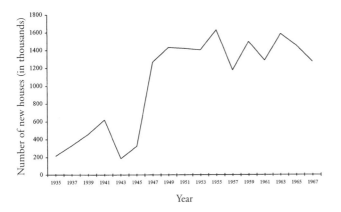

Figure 2.4. New housing starts in the United States, 1935-68. Between 1945 and 1947, housing starts in the United States grew by almost 400%. This was primarily due to the ease with which large-scale builders received financing to satisfy the post-Second World War housing demand (US Bureau of the Census 1966).

(K. Jackson 1985). A strong example of this developmental mentality was the production of the Levittown communities, as discussed in Chapter 1. These practices, in addition to mortgage guarantees provided by the FHA and VA, allowed supply of building to meet demand, so that by the mid-1940s the level of housing starts climbed steadily, as illustrated in the census statistics shown in Figure 2.4.

The now-widespread popularity of the car did little to discourage large-scale development. The US government continued to contribute to the national car dependency in 1956 with the Interstate Highway Act. The act established a trust fund through which the government paid 90% of state and local expressway construction costs. This came as a terrible blow to the American public transit system, as transit use has declined steadily since that time (Muller 1981). The presence of

the automobile has not been quite so overpowering in Canada: the US has four times as many lane miles of urban expressway per capita as Canada has, and the number of cars per capita has consistently been about 50% higher in the US than in Canada (Goldberg and Mercer 1986). Overall, Canadian cities have more viable public transportation systems than American cities, and less deterioration in the downtown cores, yet Canadian suburban development and sprawl have also been extensive.

The direct effect of the automobile on the planning of suburban subdivisions is evidenced in the switch from grid to hierarchical road networks for reasons of safety. In the mid-1950s, traffic engineering studies revealed that the accident rate was substantially higher for grid-pattern subdivisions than for limited-access subdivisions by a ratio of almost eight to one. T-intersections were found to be fourteen times safer than four-leg intersections. The Institute of Traffic Engineers (ITE, later renamed the Institute of Transportation Engineers) promoted revised standards "to establish an engineering format for the discontinuous form of subdivision layout," including limited access to the perimeter highway, discontinuous local streets to discourage through traffic, curvilinear alignment and associated design features, numerous three-leg T-intersections, and local street widths with 40- to 60-foot rights of way and 26- to 36-foot pavements (ITE 1965; Southworth and Ben-Joseph 1997). These standards are widely used as the basis for subdivision regulations; their regular use by legislatures make it difficult to implement new design approaches to suburban development.

The greatest impact of the two factors of tract development and the automobile on postwar suburbanization was the production of "bigger, more separate and dispersed congregations of similar-income groups. [As a result], the opportunity to reside among compatibly perceived neighbours and maintain social distance from others" was extended to the entire previously urban middle class (Muller 1981).

Postwar housing in Canada followed a similar, if not identical, pattern to that in the US. Returning veterans, the baby boom, transformed urban conditions, and the end of the wartime economy led to major changes in Canadian housing. Even before the end of the war, in 1944, the National Housing Act (NHA) was amended to stimulate the construction of new houses, provide for community planning, and boost employment (Wolfe 1994). Since 1945, all levels of government in Canada encouraged homeownership as "good for Canada" (Miron 1993). The federal government's involvement in the postwar housing market was both direct, with building and mortgage subsidies, and indirect, with fixed NHA mortgage rates and the protection of lending institutions against default losses. The federal government also used the residential construction industry to achieve economic objectives such as full employment, economic growth, and price stability (Poapst 1993). Guaranteed loan programs and financial assistance to meet the needs of increasing numbers of home buyers helped to ease the transition from a wartime to a peacetime economy (Colderley 1999). As a result of government involvement, in addition to changing demographics and economics, the stock of Canadian housing rose dramatically in the postwar period. Over 1 million housing units were built within ten years of the war's end. Overall, the number of total dwellings in Canada doubled (from 3 to 6 million units) in the years between 1946 and 1970 (Smith 1974).

Don Mills, Ontario (northeast of Toronto), is considered the most influential postwar suburban development in Canada: it was an economic success and its style was influential, frequently imitated (Sewell 1993). Like Levittown in the United States, Don Mills was the result of the efforts of a single entrepreneur, E.P. Taylor. Macklin Hancock was the project's innovative planner, and Taylor's skills as a businessperson and developer made the plan so successful. Don Mills was conceived in the mid-1950s as a total unit, an example of "new town," neighbourhood-based planning (Hodge 1998). Similar planning was also used in Ajax, Ontario (east of Toronto), and in Strathcona Park, Alberta (outside Edmonton). Although Don Mills was sometimes referred to as the Canadian Levittown, there were fundamental differences between the two. Don Mills was divided into four neighbourhood units, each one focused on an elementary school. A number of land uses and a variety

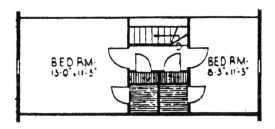

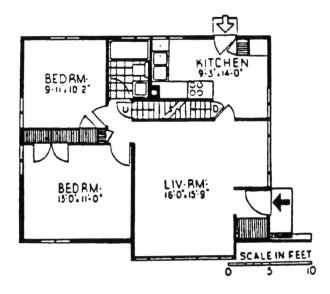

Figure 2.5. The Cape Cod floor plan allows for great flexibility with regard to multi-use space (Architectural Forum 1949). (This property will be capitalized upon in later sections, as an evaluation of augmenting the suburban housing of this period is made.)

of architectural styles were employed in the development. One-half of the 8,121 units were apartments, most of them in three-storey blocks; the other units were a mix of single-family, semi-detached, and rowhouses (Sewell 1993). Even within the single-family dwellings, special care was taken to ensure a

wide variety (Spelt 1973). The establishment of mixed land-use patterns provided the community with separate residential, commercial, institutional, and industrial zones.

In addition to the creation of large-scale developments, the attempt to meet the great housing demand of the postwar period led to new requirements for building efficiency. Prefabrication was seen as one solution. Prefabrication of entire housing units was undertaken, but it turned out to be cumbersome and uneconomical. Prefabrication strategies were also applied to various components of the home, and by 1951 one-fifth of an average house was made of prefabricated components (Friedman 1997a). Mass-produced housing had several implications, including concentration on compact and efficient design, economical construction techniques, and the need for skillful and persuasive marketing strategies. The popularity of these mass-produced houses with builders and the population of North America led to the creation of nearly instant communities and the virtual elimination of the architect from the building process.

Despite the change in design priorities that mass production led to, it can be argued that "the post-war housing crisis resulted in the application of a wealth of technological and design innovations in what traditionally had been a conservative industry" (Friedman 1997a). Ubiquitous design was a critical component of postwar housing. Strict legislation was imposed by the widely used FHA and the VA to limit the type of home that would qualify for financing. The house had to be priced between $6,000 and $8,000, and be between 80 and 110 m^2 (800 and 1,100 ft^2); for the sake of comparison, the average size of a new single-family home today is 225 m^2 (2,250 ft^2) (Friedman 1995; NAHB 2001). Such specifications demanded that homes be designed for maximum efficiency with minimum construction costs. Innovative design strategies found in postwar homes can be seen in plans of the revitalized Cape Cod cottage (80 m^2/800 ft^2), shown in Figure 2.5. They include a simple, open floor plan to permit maximum floor space with minimum wall construction, the virtual elimination of circulation space, the inclusion of multi-purpose rooms, and large plate-glass windows to enhance the feeling of spaciousness within the small home.

As opposed to the tremendous push for efficiency in design to save on building costs, a great inefficiency in land utilization caused vast suburban sprawl. Land costs were negligible, single-unit lot sizes were smaller than in the suburbs of previous eras, although the developments themselves were much larger (a comparison of community sizes and suburban lot sizes over a period of over 100 years is shown in Figure 2.6) and cars had made the continent a much smaller place. Despite these facts, the careful design considerations implemented within the homes themselves produced true models of efficiency and multi-functional space, making them desirable places to live in, even today.

The extent of change in suburban developments over the years is a result of original design flexibility (or the lack thereof) and the effect of restrictive covenants. In the United States, for example, most of the homes in Riverside have remained unchanged over the years. In addition to strong design controls, the municipality was designated a National Historic Landmark in 1970, rendering the possibility of change next to impossible. In contrast, the homes built over a century later in Levittown have been heavily modified. During the early years following the construction of his homes, when Levitt owned and rented them out, restrictive covenants in the deeds forbade changes to the houses. After Levitt sold the homes, however, the covenants expired and the new owners immediately undertook extensive modifications.

In Canada, two developments on the island of Montreal serve to highlight the difference between a municipality that has remained relatively unchanged since its construction and a suburb where the homes have been extensively modified. The idea for creating the Town of Mount Royal (TMR) as a middle-class suburb came at the end of a housing boom, in 1910, as a way by which the Canadian Northern Railway could help finance its tunnel under Mount Royal. The plan by Frederick Todd—a hybrid of both City Beautiful and Garden City principles—took the form of a grid overlaid by diagonal streets. The infrastructure was laid out by 1912 and regulatory bylaws were instituted by 1917, controlling land use, prohibiting industry, and establishing restrictive covenants (McCann 1996). Design guidelines were also set, subject to review by an architectural commission, which governed specifics such as setbacks and

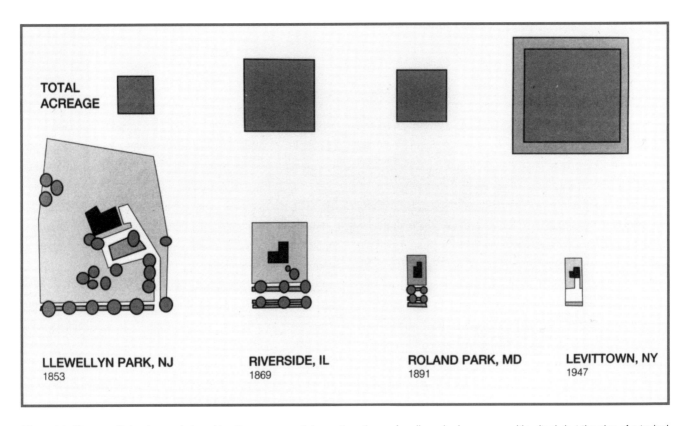

TOTAL
ACREAGE

LLEWELLYN PARK, NJ
1853

RIVERSIDE, IL
1869

ROLAND PARK, MD
1891

LEVITTOWN, NY
1947

Figure 2.6. The overall development size of Levittown was much larger than those of earlier suburban communities (top), but the size of a typical Levittown lot was much smaller than those of earlier suburban homes from the mid to late nineteenth century (bottom) (Easterling 1993).

height requirements. Although there is unity in terms of residential land use, there is great diversity in housing forms and styles, largely due to the phasing of the development. Not surprisingly, because of the restrictive covenants and design diversity, there have not been major modifications in TMR.

Cité-Jardin du Tricentaire, in the east end of Montreal, was created in 1940 by a lawyer, Auguste Gosselin, and a priest, Father Jean d'Auteuil Richard. The intent was to provide the francophone working class with a healthier environment; as such, the incentives were moral, social, and economic (Marsan 1981). Only one-quarter of the intended plan was completed, but the project was considered a success. A significant design feature is the segregation of pedestrians and cars. The diversity of housing design was limited: "Conformity of design was not only a direct result of standardization, but a conscious effort to reinforce the community's cultural homogeneity through visual conformity" (Gilliland 2000). Over the years, the original houses in Cité-Jardin have been modified extensively, notably by additions to increase the size of the home (Choko 1988). Neighbourhood covenants no longer inhibit the ability of owners to renovate their homes, but "architectural continuity has been maintained in Cité-Jardin through an informal code of community conduct" (Gilliland 2000).

Over 60% of today's housing stock in North America has been built since 1950, and the market demand has not shown signs of relenting (Muller 1981). Between 1950 and 1970, for instance, 83% of the United States' growth took place in suburbia. Beginning in the 1970s, the economics of the North American suburb began changing as, parallel to residential expansion, commercial and industrial interests moved in. In its first phase of economic reorganization, services and retailers, especially in the form of shopping malls, followed the paths of ample consumers into suburbia (Coffey 1994). The second phase saw manufacturers relocate to the fringe in search of lower land costs, taxes, and labour costs, and better transportation access, than could be found in central city locations. Between 1970 and 1980, 400,000 manufacturing jobs were lost in America's city centres, while 1.6 million were gained in the suburbs (Baldasarre 1986). The third phase of economic change was the relocation of certain "back-office" functions of central business district offices.

The 1980s saw a new wave of decentralization and an acceleration of the economic trends that had begun in the previous decade. The fact that this economic growth has occurred without significant changes in housing practice has made it difficult for employees to find residences in close proximity to their jobs, causing a greater reliance on commuting via the automobile.

The suburbs of the 1990s have begun to embrace their redefined function as the key to the expansion of metropolitan economies. Fishman (1987) refers to these new areas as "technoburbs," stressing that the basis of their economic strength is in the information-technology services sector. In some areas, these "edge cities" have become so economically strong as to actually compete with central business districts for higher-order service functions (Garreau 1991).

Such change in economic character is proof that postwar bedroom communities are no longer in step with the concept of the orthodox North American suburb. The massive decentralization of metropolitan areas that has occurred caused the suburb to augment its original meaning as a composite of urban and rural life. Arguably, it is now a new form of city. Evidence of the interdependent suburban network that forms the basis for this new city is the existence of beltways that circumvent nearly every major city on the continent though they connect suburbs to each other. The single-family home of the new suburban city is no longer conceived as a refuge but rather as a convenient base of operations. "The true centre of this new city is not in some downtown business district, but in each residential unit. From that central starting point, the members of the households create their own city from the multitude of destinations that are within a suitable driving distance" (Fishman 1987).

The notion of sustainable development, as important as it is today to planners, designers, and citizens, was an unknown and irrelevant consideration to suburban builders of the immediate postwar period. In their 1986 work, *Sustainable Communities*, Sim Van der Ryn and Peter Calthorpe propose eight basic principles that, when attended to, can create a healthier, more sustainable suburban development. They are: (1) designing with a greater-than-standard residential housing density, (2) locating shopping and service amenities locally, (3) building a local employment base within the community, (4) implementing energy- and information-efficient building strategies, (5) designing to encourage the emergence of local social networks, (6) providing local energy and food production, (7) recycling wastes and water, and (8) integrating community design with a balanced transportation system.

These eight principles are meant to create a "village settlement," as Van der Ryn and Calthorpe call it, rather than a bedroom community. The village has space for homes, work, and amenities, while a bedroom community is a homogeneous residential development. The village is, to a great extent, autonomous, defined by its own economy and social structures. Tom Daniels, in *When City and Country Collide* (1999), proposes that "a village has a human scale; a fairly dense settlement pattern; and social, architectural, and economic

cohesion." As such, this concept of the village settlement has been adopted as an ideal model by the New Urbanism movement of the 1990s.

In 1991, a committee (consisting mainly of New Urbanists) at a seminar in the Ahwahnee Hotel in Yosemite National Park laid out a series of principles intended to address problematic issues in current regional and community planning. The community principles, influenced heavily by Van der Ryn and Calthorpe's principles, are: (1) planning should be in the form of integrated communities containing housing, shops, workplace, schools, parks, and civic facilities; (2) community size should be designed so that housing, jobs, daily needs, and other activities are within easy walking distance of each other; (3) as many activities as possible should be located within easy walking distance of transit stops; (4) a community should contain a diversity of housing types to enable citizens from a wide range of economic levels and age groups to live within it; (5) the location and character of the community should be consistent with a larger transit network; (6) the community should have a central focus that combines commercial, civic, cultural, and recreational uses; (7) the community should contain an ample supply of specialized open space in the form of squares, greens, and parks; (8) each community or cluster of communities should have a well-defined edge, such as agricultural greenbelts or wildlife corridors, permanently protected from development; (9) streets, pedestrian paths, and bike paths should contribute to a system of fully connected routes to all destinations; and (10) the community design should help conserve resources and minimize waste.

With the transformation of social circumstances (for example, a change in middle-class tastes, the degradation of urban life, or the ending of a war), development patterns and ideals shift as well. Though the character of suburbia is rapidly changing, little change has been made in the way of built form or unit design to accommodate this change. The following chapter considers several contemporary precedent developments. In these examples, a philosophical framework is established by which the dynamics of a new suburbia can be properly addressed. The strengths of those precedents will be assimilated into the proposed planning methods and ideals outlined in the later sections of this book.

Designing Flexible Outgrowth:
Precedent Models

Responding to the dynamics of our urban centres and suburbs by constantly revising the process of development and the manner in which we interpret the ideal living condition is not new. The previous chapter has shown that the theories that have shaped our suburban form are largely the result of repeated reconsideration of how Western society should live in settlement. Few, if any, theoreticians have formulated their opinions and designs without having keen hindsight as an adjunct to less reliable foresight. In other words, nobody starts with a clean slate.

With regard to planning and designing the North American suburb in order to accommodate change, the philosophy that shall be proposed in this book is no different. There have been numerous prior attempts to address effectively the shifting nature of the suburban condition and hypothesize the best method for handling future change. In fact, as the continental blight of "suburban sprawl" has refused to abate, these theories have come into high demand. An understanding of the existing "philosophy of flexibility" is therefore imperative, in order to fully appreciate the proposed theory as it has been applied experimentally and as the next step in the re-evaluation of suburban design theory.

Christopher Alexander's collaborative work *A New Theory of Urban Design* (1987) outlines processes for the development of brand-new communities and offers a wealth of ideas that are applicable and relevant to the transformation of existing developments. Alexander identifies characteristics of traditional cities that render them superior in visual and experiential quality to their modern, pre-packaged, pre-planned counterparts. He also attempts to articulate the essential characteristics common to all successful urban outgrowth.

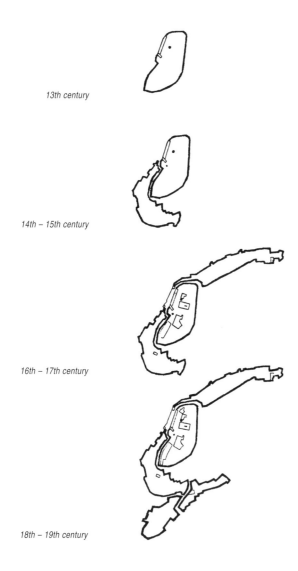

13th century

14th – 15th century

16th – 17th century

18th – 19th century

Figure 3.1. Alexander proposes that when a city grows in a piecemeal fashion its character is automatically informed by the character of the existing structure. In this manner, wholeness is maintained (Alexander et al. 1987).

The traditional growth of cities, he maintains, occurred in a piecemeal fashion over a very broad time period, as can be seen in the growth of a hill town in Figure 3.1. Such an evolution permitted cities to grow only incrementally at their limits, and at a slow pace. This gradual addition allowed for new construction that maintained the character of the city and contributed to developing such character.

The word Alexander utilizes to describe his concept of unified growth and the spirit of all successful places is *wholeness*: "A thing is whole according to how free it is of inner contradictions" (Alexander 1979). Wholeness, per se, is a difficult quality to define. Elsewhere, Alexander writes that it occurs when new growth emerges from the "specific, peculiar structural nature of its past," and that "whole grows piecemeal, whole is unpredictable, whole is coherent, whole is full of feeling" (Alexander et al. 1987). Alexander proposes that the wholeness of a community should be shielded from guidelines and controls that would restrict its pervasive though somewhat nebulous powers.

Though challenging, wholeness connotes a positive unification, however difficult to quantify. Alexander acknowledges this difficulty himself as a component inevitable to a theory that explores such a vast goal. The fundamental element of this generative theory is that each act of construction performed in a community must work to heal it by creating wholes—complete entities. The meaning becomes more apparent when considered in reverse. Urban problems are the result of an imbalanced application of pressures. Certain elements are overemphasized (rush-hour traffic circulation, for instance); certain elements are underemphasized (opportunities for casual socialization). (Jan Gehl, in *Life Between Buildings* [1987], divides all outdoor activities into three types— necessary, optional, and social—with each type placing a different demand on the physical environment.) This lack of equilibrium destroys the notion of wholeness in interrelations between community activities. Alexander offers a critically opposed viewpoint: the elements of urban growth should be integrated as parts to a single whole. Where he fails to generate accord with prototypical logic, Alexander resorts to a more innate perception of wholeness: "although wholeness is hard to define and evokes so many discussions—still most people have a rather good intuitive sense of what it means. It is therefore a very useful kind of inner voice, which forces people to pay attention to the balance between different goals and to put things together in a balanced fashion" (Alexander et al. 1987). These theories place a great deal of faith on the intuition and personal decisions made by individuals, in lieu of the imposition of an omnipotent, inflexible "master plan." Additionally, the theory recognizes that developmental decisions are context-specific, rather than dependent upon an arbitrary, predetermined agenda.

In addition to wholeness, this theory proposes a set of seven urban issues that must be addressed in new built form. The seven were developed as a result of Alexander's research, analysis, and experimentation at the University of California at Berkeley in 1978. The seven issues pertain to those aspects that contribute to the structural quality of "beautiful old towns." They are piecemeal growth, growth of larger wholes, vision, basic rules of positive urban space, layout of large buildings, construction, and formation of centres.

Alexander acknowledges that these are not novel points but that they collectively form the foundation of architectural heritage as it has been known for centuries. Taken together they are therefore presently applicable on a large scale. The novelty in this approach is the presentation and integration of such plain material. This theory is unique in the manner in which these ingredients are offered as a recipe contrary to common planning practices for urban outgrowth. The interlocking of generated whole entities at many scales generates a hierarchical diversity of the urban structure.

Addressing the seven issues of growth allows for a great flexibility. Guaranteeing piecemeal growth ensures that the planning of new urban development will not supersede the rate of actual demanded development. Even on the scale of a rapidly expanding metropolis (much larger, obviously, than a hill town), growth will therefore reflect the contemporary circumstances of its society and maintain a harmony parallel to economic and demographic demands. The open-ended nature of this theory's approach, its loose definitions and implied meanings, and the factors that contribute to its flexibility are what leave it open to criticism. Perhaps because of the youth of this theory, it does not engage conventional practices or accepted norms. Its point of departure is one that disregards current planning procedure as failures—unworthy of consideration. This assumption may well be intellectually defensible but it reduces the applicability of the entire theory and leaves it in a highly theoretical form.

In his article entitled "Emerging Urban Spaces in the Suburbs" (1989), Thomas Emodi is critical of the condescending attitudes architects sometimes express towards the suburbs. In contrast, he views the existing suburbs as an accessible petri dish in which innovative experiments in urban living can be conducted. He refutes the assertion that there is no community life in the contemporary suburb by specifying three public activities that embody such life: residential street use, public institution function, and commercial centre (shopping mall) activity. However, the manner in which the suburbs are presently segregated prevents the integration of these three elements into a complete communal entity and prevents a suburban vitality. His theory also acknowledges the extent to which commercial activity has been removed from residential settings through an asphalt isolation. Emodi considers commercial life an integral cultural element that should be physically tied to civic life.

According to this theory, the two key barriers that prevent a rich suburban complex are low density and a lack of variety of activity. The theory approaches these obstacles as a component of the existing condition—the first and not the final layer of development. Strategies of infill development are proposed to combat existing problems. With the addition of small-scale commercial activity and alternative residential forms, the density would be increased and the variety and vitality would accordingly flourish. Emodi sensibly recommends the adoption of "a strategy that addresses the problems, but also preserves the desirable qualities of suburban life" (Emodi 1989). These qualities are the freedom, privacy, and control associated with the single-family lot, and also such basic suburban benefits as access to fresh air and open space.

The strength of Emodi's proposal is the recognition of the potential for development in the existing suburbs. However, it seems that in treating suburbia as a faceless entity—simply a pattern of land use—there has been missed opportunity in the treatment of context, something that Alexander's theory was intensely focused upon. Emodi's theory also fails to distinguish clearly between new development and the transformation of an existing form. Despite citing "cultural and ecological" justification for the reconfiguration of the suburbs, this theory disregards the unique role that the current inhabitants of these areas play. Their needs and actions will ultimately determine what form future growth will adopt.

Similarly, in an article entitled "Suburban Intensification" (1989), Greenberg advocates the transformation of existing suburbs. The two goals in his theory are to create true public spaces and enable parts of suburban areas "to become truly urban." While the former goal is almost irrefutable, the latter is perhaps unrealistic and widely inapplicable, if not totally inappropriate. The argument Greenberg makes is that, from a Canadian perspective, urban areas are not feared or resisted as they are in the United States. Rather, new urbanity would be a welcome addition to the sterility of the suburbs (this is the attitude that Emodi considers to be counterproductive in his article mentioned previously). Greenberg's image of the city core as a place of "richness, variety, amenity, walking environment and intricacy" is a romantic one, though admittedly these qualities would enliven suburban neighbourhoods considerably.

The evolutionary transition as it is proposed to turn the suburban into the urban is intriguing. Greenberg's theory recognizes the error in viewing projects in isolation—as complete unto themselves—and an appeal is made for new urban structures to saturate existing voids and enhance the texture of the suburban environment. He criticizes suburban building for having "to address two time frames—present that is still fundamentally suburban in operation and a future that will be more urban" (Greenberg 1989). Also noted is the role of reconfiguring streets in order to create smaller blocks, greater alternatives for traffic flow, and walkable sidewalks, which would presumably reduce the current privatization of public life.

Though they are somewhat extreme, Greenberg's urbanization principles and recognition of a potential suburban evolution process are important in addressing an effective solution to the contemporary weakened suburban condition.

A more common approach to dealing with the outgrowth of cities is to lay out a specific urban design and allow for lateral movement within that prescribed fabric. By this methodology, the city is designated as a multiple of a particular pattern. Any new growth of the city would occur along parameters provided by the existing urban pattern—it would be a recurrence of the same. This philosophy has been realized by two Israeli architects, Al Mansfeld and Salo Hershman (no doubt because of the tremendous influx of immigration that Israel is currently experiencing and the great demand for new housing development). Both architects consider incremental growth as a basis for their urban planning and utilize complete modules to propagate such growth. Mansfeld's buildings and suburban designs are composed of constituent modules, with the intention that the resulting system would have an inherent flexibility in its size and boundaries and would fluctuate according to market conditions without compromising the integrity of the generated structure.

To process this notion of flexible growth, a framework must inform the location and combination of additional modular components in order to avoid haphazard expansion. And there must be a minimum size of the urban cluster in order to generate and sustain the demands of a community. Mansfeld develops a concept of urban outgrowth that also governs the overall character of the city's boundaries. Rather than assigning concentric growth at the edge of a city, Mansfeld proposes ring roads, shown in Figure 3.2, that radiate from the edge of the city in a loop and eventually connect back with it. Outgrowth is accommodated by such roads rather than encouraged immediately adjacent to the city's limits.

In a 1973 project in Haifa, Shaar Ha'aliya, Mansfeld succeeded in establishing a flexible pattern for development by laying out the framework that would guide subsequent forms and relationships within the development without designating them specifically. He represented such a foundation as a graphically illustrated, predetermined urban pattern, an example of which is seen in Figure 3.3. Buildings were indicated by simple rectangles, coded to represent a density level and a particular building element. Arranged adjacent to one another rectilinearly, these configurations took advantage of a wide range of densities to create a landscape in a mildly restrictive linear pattern. The possible addition of new buildings at the edge of this urban form was provided for in accordance with the precedent density relationships established from the outset of the project. Urban fabric should thus evolve as a chain of linked buildings related to a larger whole, though without a finite definition of this chain. Here, Mansfeld incorporated flexibility to accommodate a fluctuating community size (Mansfeld 1975).

Salo Hershman approaches the concept of establishing a predetermined pattern similarly, though with a more rigidly structured repetitive geometry. Where Mansfeld's intention was to create interest and variety through the integration of a set of repeated building types in a semi-organic manner, Hershman actually dictates this pattern in an explicit, almost molecular manner, in terms of repetition, uniformity, and the homogeneity of individual components and their identical interrelationships, as seen in Figure 3.4. This formal simplicity, however, masks an underlying richness in the complexity of transportation and community networks. A pattern of octagonal building elements is superimposed upon a grid pattern of vehicular circulation. This is what generated the spatial hierarchy within the urban fabric, as proposed by Hershman (1975).

Such an overall form is easily analogous to an intricate tapestry, woven of many elements that together form a balanced and complete whole. All the constituents of an urban community are accounted for in this woven geometry. Vehicular and pedestrian circulation are included, as well as open and recreational space. The result is precisely calculated from a formula that anticipates expansion as an application of these individual geometric modules in any direction. The city becomes a cellular organism. It is permitted to grow indefinitely according to increments of the prescribed module. This octagonal system is reminiscent of the street pattern based

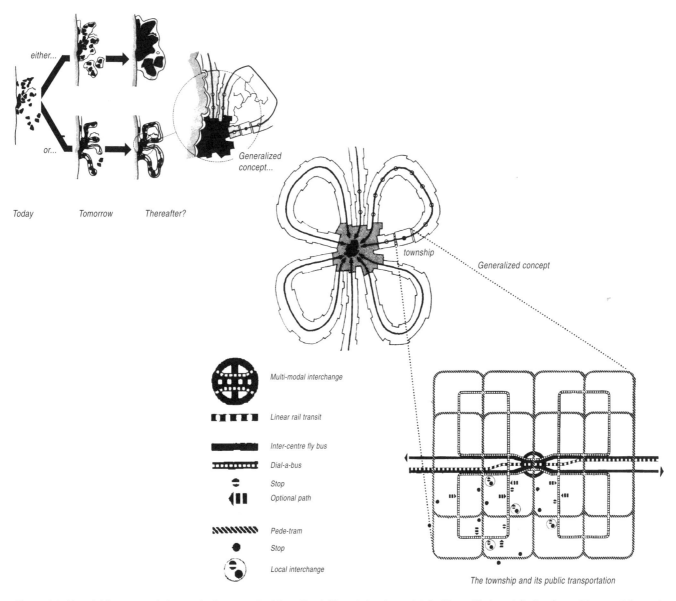

either...

or...

Today   *Tomorrow*   *Thereafter?*

Generalized concept...

township

Generalized concept

Multi-modal interchange

Linear rail transit

Inter-centre fly bus

Dial-a-bus

Stop

Optional path

Pede-tram

Stop

Local interchange

The township and its public transportation

Figure 3.2. Mansfeld's proposed ring roads, in conceptual form (top left) and showing a detail of township layout (bottom), would prevent the sort of random, radiating city sprawl that is common today. Suburban residents are guaranteed easy access to the countryside and, via the main loop artery, to the city (Mansfeld 1975).

Model showing variations of heights and volumes

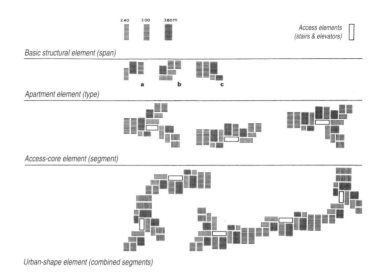

240   300   380m

Access elements
(stairs & elevators)

Basic structural element (span)

a   b   c

Apartment element (type)

Access-core element (segment)

Urban-shape element (combined segments)

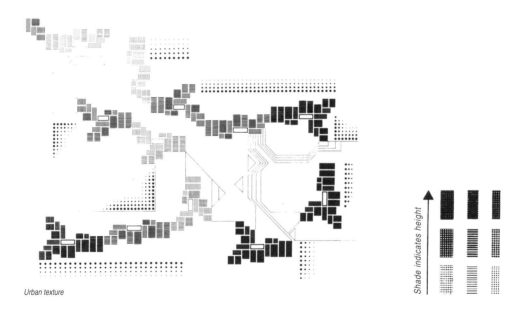

Urban texture

Shade indicates height

Figure 3.3. For a development in Haifa, Mansfeld wove an urban fabric based on unorthodox planning criteria. With an idea of what the composite whole should look like, Mansfeld assigned densities and building elements in a way that allows for healthy, mixed neighbourhoods (Mansfeld 1975).

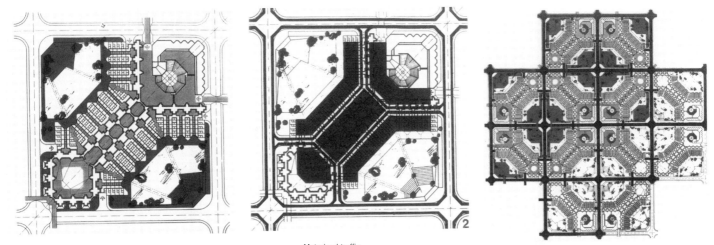

Pedestrian network

Motorized traffic

Network of the urban sector traffic and destination schemes

Model showing neighborhood expansion based on Hershman's principles

Figure 3.4. With a strict repetitive geometry, not unlike the concepts developed by earlier urban reformers, Hershman's design provides separate patterns for vehicular and pedestrian traffic. Also, housing is provided for at the perimeter of the diamond-shaped block, adjacent to the open green space at the interior (Hershman 1975).

upon hexagonal blocks, proposed by planners such as Charles Lamb, Noulan Cauchon, and Barry Parker in North America during the first three and a half decades of the twentieth century; this pattern never gained widespread acceptability and was displaced in the mid-1930s by the neighbourhood unit of cul-de-sacs and loops (Ben-Joseph and Gordon 2000).

Both Hershman's and Mansfeld's works share a common shortcoming in their vision of what gradual outgrowth means. Though Mansfeld's approach lends itself to greater freedom in the individual adherence to the general pattern, both architects have designed a system that would perpetuate only itself. The pattern would continue indefinitely. Despite being—or perhaps because they are—the products of careful research and calculation, these two philosophies are dogmatic in approach. The pattern assumes that it is a complete end, representative of society's needs. Following this assumption is the implication that the progression of community needs through time will be consistent with the original applications of these forms. Can urban form remain immune to the natural dynamics of North American or Israeli society and culture? Not likely. However thorough and physically flexible the geometry these theories propose, they are dated and therefore temporally inflexible.

With the exception of Alexander et al.'s *A New Theory of Urban Design*, the projects presented seem rather myopic in their approach. Idiosyncratic and self-perpetuating, they assume that the planned pattern as laid out in the present will continue to be relevant into the future, regardless of the changes that take place around it. Of course, Alexander's theory sidesteps the trap of dogmatism by suggesting tactics and characteristics rather than dictating specifics, and winds up losing touch with the realities of current planning and developmental procedures.

Much of current North American practice is based upon the neighbourhood unit, laid out within the context of a rectangular or square grid established by nineteenth-century land surveys. In 1929, architect Clarence Perry created the concept of the neighbourhood unit that would eventually become "one of the strongest physical organizing principles in modern community plans" (Hodge 1998). Its use as a planning principle resulted from the attempt to find a "workable unit of human scale around which housing and community services could be organized and designed" (Hodge 1998). The neighbourhood unit was created to satisfy the objectives of pedestrian safety, efficient service provision, and the building of community.

Although its exact shape was not specified, Perry's neighbourhood unit was defined precisely. The idea was to link residential areas, each about 64 hectares (160 acres or a quarter of a square mile) in size, or large enough to house enough people to require one elementary school, with a distance of about 500 m (1,650 ft) from each home to its corresponding school. The total population of a neighbourhood unit would be 1,500 families or 5,000 to 6,000 people. The issue of transportation was vital to the plan; it was devised at a time when automobile usage and its dangers were rising, so main streets would be planned to surround the unit rather than pass through it (Hodge 1998; Perry 1929).

During his time and up to this day, Perry's neighbourhood unit has not been without its critics. Opponents to the plan have argued that spatial units could neither encompass nor promote a cohesive social environment (Hodge 1998). Considered a "planning illusion," the neighbourhood unit is a cellular construct, whereas "any good city has a continuous fabric" (Lynch 1981). Although Perry's concept was even said to border on social engineering, the plan and its contemporary incarnations have been widely used.

The approach of the New Urbanists to development (discussed in Chapter 1, under the topic of Seaside, Florida) displays a modified version of the neighbourhood unit plan. The Charter of the New Urbanism echoes some of Perry's principles: neighbourhoods should be "compact, pedestrian-friendly, and mixed-use," and the concentrations of "civic, institutional, and commercial activity should be embedded in neighborhoods and districts" (CNU 2001). Borrowing from other planning traditions as well, New Urbanists design communities to be held together by the human element and recognize the demand for convenient travel (Ryan and McNally 1995). Significantly, the Charter of the New Urbanism includes a mention of design codes to guide the evolution of communities, although details are lacking: "The economic health and harmonious evolution of neighborhoods, districts, and corridors can be improved through graphic urban design codes that serve as predictable guides for change" (CNU 2001).

The projects and theories that have been presented in this chapter are not totally inclusive of the planning procedures that have been developed to address the issues of growth, change, and flexibility. They are, however, indicative of the kinds of solutions that are necessary, as well as of the limitations of such solutions.

A solution that would bridge the gap between dogmatic realism and cloudy flexibility should have enough vision to be open-ended yet pragmatic enough to set out specific guidelines that are quickly discernible and communicable. The goal is to create controls that are guiding yet flexible, and to bear in mind the inherent limitations in trying to predict variables that are currently unknown.

The developers who built the suburbs of North America, especially the earlier suburbs, realized that they had found a commodity with wide appeal. This commodity was autonomous existence, on individual lots, in a personalized environment, within easy reach of employment, nature, and cultural and recreational activities. These features still exist today in mature suburbs. Accompanied by a settled, quaint architecture and a full landscape, such neighbourhoods continue to be attractive places in which to live. Based on demographic trends and shifting economic climate, however, these communities are facing pressures to change.

The driving principle behind the theory to be proposed in this book is that future evolution of mature suburban communities must play a dual role: maintaining the character of the community while ushering in the necessary changes. The contribution that this book makes to this process is the suggestion of a method for controlling change that will enable such a neighbourhood to move into the future in a healthy, positive manner. The goal is not to superimpose something on an existing site but to provide a well-planned framework through which change can be articulated and therefore contribute to the wholeness of a community rather than detract from it.

Several broad aspects of the mature suburb must be addressed in order to bring about a graceful temporal transition of development character. First is the problem of limited housing types available. As previously discussed, the earliest function of suburbia was that of a haven for the wealthy, away from the grime of the city. The role that society asks early suburbs to play at the threshold of the twenty-first century, however, is quite different from this intent. Suburbia, from the post-Second World War era onward, has meant the attainment of a haven for the entire middle class. As Fishman, in his 1987 work entitled *Bourgeois Utopias* notes, "how can a form based on the principle of exclusion include everyone?" In fact, the suburban form is rigidly defined by single-family detached homes on individual lots—a form that now cannot include everyone.

The lack of housing options is a serious threat to the mature suburb's sense of community. Langdon, in *A Better Place to Live* (1994), makes the comparison between a strong community and a strong immune system. A strong community enables one to fight off the effects of damaging contaminants such as an unstable economy, rampant materialism, employment insecurity, and global crises. It provides a safety net for its residents by silently, consistently providing them with a supportive environment in which to live. Suburbs that offer only one type of housing cannot readily accommodate changes in the lives of its residents; as a result, when change does occur, individuals are forced to weaken the community by leaving it or living in inappropriate housing. A strong community anticipates and embraces peoples' differences and allows for the most fulfilling and appropriate lifestyle possible.

Another aspect of suburbia that should be addressed is the provision or maintenance of community centres, in order to provide a reason to feel unified as a community for what may otherwise be an unfocused place. Additionally, the continuing growth of the non-residential economic environment brings a greater quantity of traffic into residential areas. This leaves residents feeling as if they have been relegated to secondary space—the land left over between roads. Steps towards maintaining human scale must be taken in order to ensure that residents still feel a part of their environment.

Perhaps the most domineering aspect of suburbia is the archaic developmental regulations that govern the form in which suburbs exist. These regulations must be addressed in order to create a more resident-friendly, adaptable suburb. Zoning ordinances enacted decades ago—which, for example, demand extremely low densities, restrict the definition of "single-family," and make no provisions for working at home— will prevent former "bedroom communities" from successfully meeting the demands of its future residents.

The philosophy whereby individuals live in isolation from their neighbours and follow a daily routine that revolves around the family car is fading. In its place, the desire for a community-oriented environment is growing. Unfortunately, the current process of urban planning is both a product of and a vehicle for the stifling effects of obsolete, misguided development regulations. Planners who would like to respond to this new community awareness through creative, dynamic design are too often limited by the inflexibility of control mechanisms that must be adhered to (even at the expense of good judgment). There is an immediate need for the reform of development regulations to allow planners flexibility so that they can integrate the complexities of modern society into an established environment. Flexibility in regulations is required both to accommodate new ways of living at present and to enable future planners to adapt to the times ahead.

Since existing neighbourhoods are frequently mummified by their current regulations, planners turn to new developments in an attempt to correct the mistakes of the past. They begin, though, with one strike against them, even before the first drawing is made or the first house is built. In planning on fresh land at the periphery of an existing development, the final product, no matter the ingenuity of the plan, is invariably sprawl. What we propose, therefore, is a method for planning where the problems already exist.

A fundamental part of the proposed planning process is the definition of a "vision" of future developmental activity. In this respect, there is little difference from traditional planning. The fact that this new "vision" is built upon the base of an existing community is where the novelty of the plan appears. The proposed approach also varies from traditional planning by the augmentation of typical development controls. The intent is not, however, to make change simply for the sake of change. Rather, in keeping with the spirit of Alexander et al.'s *A New Theory of Urban Design*, the proposed process is an approach to replanning an existing suburban site with the goal of making it more "whole." It is, hopefully, a thought process that can be applied to many suburban areas, though it is understood that

each existing subdivision has a life of its own. After decades of existence, mature suburban communities have a character and context that must be respected. Consequently, the current proposal presents a process for reconfiguring a specific place in the image of what it was and what it is desired to become. It also acknowledges that in North America's material culture, property value is a primary issue, and therefore an

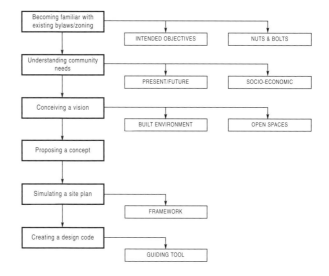

Figure 4.1. At the beginning, the six-step planning procedure by which more responsive housing can be integrated into an existing neighbourhood requires an understanding of the particular context of the treated area. In later steps, site plans and design codes are developed based on this understanding.

understanding of human social behaviour (what is acceptable or not acceptable to a collective) must be the foundation of any conceptual-level thought.

There are six overlapping, sequential phases in the proposed planning process. Their progression and component parts are illustrated in Figure 4.1.

Step 1: Becoming Familiar with Existing Bylaws/Zoning

The process of introducing change into an existing community begins with a clear understanding of the existing mechanisms that are applicable to the site. In addition to the nuts and bolts of the rules, a comprehension of the control mechanisms' objectives is necessary; this legislation frames the structure of the existing community and is therefore the foundation on which change can be built.

Existing legislation can of course be handled in one of two ways. The old rules can be either replaced or altered within their existing structures. Determining which course should be chosen requires a deep analysis of such rules, to ascertain which elements are obsolete and which are repairable. Generally, there are design ideas at the core of bylaws and regulations, but frequently theses ideas are older and, at times, irrelevant. The fundamental nature of the current regulatory process is the cause of this obsolescence, since regulations tend to strive for comprehensiveness and will rely on standards that had been created previously. Lynch (1984) maintains that "the great majority of environmental designs are incremental adaptations of solutions previously used, especially those that have been used often enough to become stereotypes ... the cul-de-sac, the backyard, foundation planting, the street tree, the park of trees and grass, the axial vista." Hodge (1998) points out that many urban forms, such as the neighbourhood concept, are now customarily applied in urban design. In the 1930s and 1940s, many elements of the Federal Housing Administration (FHA) guidelines were inspired by features of the Radburn plan (neighbourhood units, crescents, and cul-de-sacs) by Stein and Wright; Thomas Adams, who advised both the Canadian and American federal governments, included the Radburn plan in his reports and textbooks (Ben-Joseph and Gordon 2000). Many suburban zoning bylaws that followed the economic and planning success of Don Mills were based on the Toronto suburb; by the 1970s, the planning of "every Canadian city was dominated by the suburban form espoused" by Don Mills (Sewell 1993).

Guidelines and standards lag behind the reality of the marketplace and can result in insufficient planning and development. While standards "can of course help prevent the worst creativity, they can also stifle creativity and inhibit adaptation to local situations" (Southworth and Ben-Joseph 1997). The development of explicit yet variable standards is keenly to be desired. Clearly, the more the existing mechanisms are altered, the more involved the intervention to the existing community and the more difficult it will be to implement alterations. It is beneficial to build on the strengths of the existing regulations as much as possible, making only necessary changes rather than reinventing the wheel.

Duany et al. (2000) suggest that "the best way to thoroughly upgrade a development code is to start from scratch," but point out that "the problem lies not in creating a new ordinance but in throwing out the old one." They explain that since the value of private property is determined very much by zoning, "any modification of the status quo may have profound economic consequences." Their idea is "to keep the old code intact, while offering the new code as a parallel alternative." They view existing zoning ordinances as impediments to the achievement of more urbane communities and as agents of segregation, while they should serve to connect, aggregate, and unify. Their different alternative codes include: a regulating plan, to identify streets types, public tracts reserved for squares, parks, and civic buildings, and the arrangement of private lots and corresponding building types; urban regulations, to regulate aspects of private building types, dealing with frontage, parking, and social issues; architectural regulations, to regulate materials and construction techniques, intended to produce a harmonious relationship; street types, to depict the character of the public spaces; and, finally, landscape regulations (Duany and Plater-Zyberk 1991).

Step 2: Understanding Community Needs

In planning for the evolution of a mature suburb, it is critical to become aware of the community's needs. Great care should be exercised in doing so, as there is often a discrepancy between a professional perception of what a community will need in the future and the idea that residents have for themselves. It is often a combination of these two perceptions that acts as a guide for change in a community. As a result, change will be unique for each neighbourhood.

Community needs can frequently be directly translated into regulatory reform. For example, making garden suites permissible in a community's control legislation could be the response to a demographic change such as a rise in the number of elderly households in an area. Similarly, economic issues such as downsizing of a large local corporation may result in a demand for home office zoning allowances.

Step 3: Conceiving a Vision

The process of establishing and formalizing the vision of an existing suburb demands a keen analysis by the planner. Though the concept of change was once considered incompatible with community planning, as is explicitly expressed in the inflexible ordinances that have thoroughly retarded community evolution in North America, in considering community vision it is useful to imagine the ideal neighbourhood in five, ten, or twenty years. Then it is a matter of determining the steps that must be taken along the way to bring about this desired future state.

There are three fundamental elements that, in combination, create this vision. The first is the consideration of the built environment, including functional issues of density, building use, and residence types, as well as visual concerns. The second element is the open space in the neighbourhood. A planner must consider its use, scale, appearance, and ambience, and the territorial concerns of public versus private space. Finally, the element of circulation and parking cannot be overlooked. It is likely that as fuel becomes increasingly and prohibitively expensive, there will be radical changes in the transportation practices of North America. Such transformations must be considered, though the current reliance on widespread automobile use in suburbia must be skilfully incorporated into the community vision.

Step 4: Proposing a Concept

Based upon the goals of planners and the community, an outline of specific objectives to be addressed on the way to achieving community vision can be formulated. By considering the three elements discussed in Step 3, the conceptual goal of the vision can be translated into a structure of concrete ideas. Again, this process is not one of imposing wholesale change on a neighbourhood. Rather, the planning should pave the way for changes to occur only as change is demanded. It will therefore not disrupt the existing character of the community.

Step 5: Simulating a Site Plan

The objectives established during Step 4 can now be translated into a detailed site plan. In this visual plan, the use patterns and structure of the existing neighbourhoods

become clear as the physical implications of the future vision of the neighbourhood are superimposed upon them. All three elements of the vision must be addressed on the site plan, allowing for a better understanding of the way they will evolve and affect one another. Though the site plan offers opportunities for a concrete visualization of change, it is important to remember that this proposal is a process for guiding change, not forcing it. Many future modifications can only be surmised, and therefore the site plan remains in many ways hypothetical. Nonetheless, as a vehicle for examining the paths that development may take, a carefully made and informed site plan is invaluable.

Step 6: Creating a Design Code

The final step is to formalize the envisioned process of change into a body of guiding regulations. As previously discussed, the purpose of current regulations is often to prevent change and preserve the status quo. It follows that a new planning philosophy requires new regulatory mechanisms. Though instituting a design code containing all of the ideas previously discussed is the most straightforward approach, one that acts in conjunction with the existing controls is the most practical and non-invasive way of achieving the intent of the new planning. If the existing regulations can be implemented in a positive way, as a source of attractive characteristics of a mature, though changing, neighbourhood, and are not in conflict with the goals that have been proposed, they should remain intact.

The new code, expressed graphically and verbally, must be precise in its articulation, intent, and jurisdiction. Progress that follows the "spirit of the law" should not be in violation of the "letter of the law," as is sometimes the case with current legislation. And a successful code regulates only issues that truly influence the character of the neighbourhood. At its core, the purpose of the code is to provide a guideline for desired future change. Communities should no longer fear the future and act to defend themselves from it; they should be empowered by change, embrace it, and be improved by it.

The Experiment Site: Sector 102 of Notre-Dame-de-Grâce

The area that is known as Notre-Dame-de-Grâce (NDG) began as an agricultural area west of the colonial city of Montreal. Its location on the island is highlighted in Figure 4.2. Its settlement began in the mid-1600s to improve defence and provide produce for Montreal, earning it the nickname "Montreal's Orchard" (Hanna and Charlton 1985). The early village of NDG was home to farmers and several well-off families who also maintained residence in the city.

In 1853, Notre-Dame-de-Grâce church was built, giving the area its official name. In 1910, NDG was annexed by the city of Montreal, and the wheels of its suburban development were set in motion. Montreal's electric tramlines were extended to the west, and the pleasant area quickly attracted city dwellers. The population of NDG grew rapidly—from a sparse 5,000 in 1914

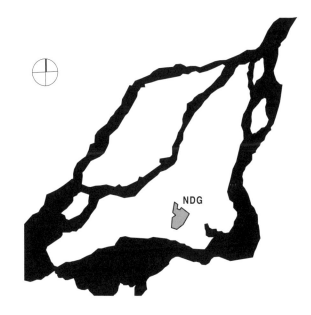

Figure 4.2. The present-day area of Notre-Dame-de-Grâce is located west and inland of the original colonial city. Initially agricultural, it became a popular suburban area early in the twentieth century.

to a bustling 50,000 by the late 1930s. After the Second World War, the baby boom and the decentralization trends, which swelled suburban populations across North America, similarly affected NDG. The population gradually became anglophone through the 1940s and 1950s, when much of NDG was built to accommodate veterans' families. By the early 1960s, neighbourhoods were filled with housing and Notre-Dame-de-Grâce began to mature as a complete community. Today, it is home to a varied population of nearly 70,000 and remains one of the most pleasant residential areas in Montreal.

The housing that can be found in NDG is indicative of its long and varied history. In its early days, when apple orchards and melon fields were more numerous than people, its inhabitants lived primarily in wooden houses set among the rolling hills. The main streets of NDG still carry the names of the farm roads they once were. As the area became home to some of Montreal's wealthier families, the architectural standards of the area began to rise, as did real estate and housing costs. The introduction of public transportation following the turn of the century increased the area's volume of house building and brought with it larger-scale, higher-density development. From about 1910 onward, housing in NDG was almost totally developer-built, and there is therefore a certain consistency to the housing built at this time. Though a variety of housing types do appear in NDG, such as the detached single-family house, the duplex, and low-rise apartment buildings, the most popular style was the semi-detached house. The architectural styles that can be found in the area are varied, according to the tastes of the household; styles range from Tudor to Georgian to Italianate. Complementing the architecture, folk art, such as decorative brickwork, stained glass, and pressed metal parapets, is common. It is interesting to note that typical Montreal housing—the three-storey plex rowhouse with a brick facade, flat roof, and exterior stair—is rare in NDG. NDG residents considered the exterior stairs tacky, and zoning prohibited them. The postwar boom continued housing production in the form of Cape Cod single-family houses, duplexes, and apartment buildings.

Figure 4.3. Most of the homes in the study site are single-family houses in the modified Cape Cod style.

The houses in the experimental site, sector 102, were built, with few exceptions, during the early 1940s and the postwar years. They are typical "modified Cape Cod" style single-family dwellings of red brick with black asphalt shingle roofs and no basement (Figure 4.3). Modifications have been made to a few of the original homes, such as adding decks, dormers, sunrooms, or, most commonly, garages. In NDG today, high-rise apartments are liberally interspersed with other housing types. Buildings higher than five storeys accommodate 18% of the population. There is very little possibility for new development in NDG at present, as it is considered saturated by today's controlling regulations.

There are a few socio-demographic characteristics that, compared with the city of Montreal and the rest of NDG, give an accurate picture of the neighbourhood—sector 102—under discussion. These statistics are based upon the 1996 census (Statistics Canada 2000, 1999; CLSC NDG/Montréal-Ouest 2000).

The total population of NDG declined from 1991 to 1996; in the same time period, the population of sector 102 also fell (Figure 4.4). In both NDG and Montreal, women outnumber men. Sector 102 has one of the lowest ratios of men to women in NDG, counting only 83 men per 100 women. The largest age group in NDG is made up of residents between 45 and 64. NDG has a slightly higher percentage of elderly residents than Montreal as a whole; sector 102 has a concentration of elderly people of 16%, as seen in Figure 4.5.

In NDG, 34% of households have no children, while in sector 102 this figure jumps to 44%. It is significant that one-third of all families in NDG are single-parent families, higher than the proportion for Montreal as a whole (Figure 4.6). The proportion of single-parent families in NDG, by sector, is illustrated in Figure 4.7.

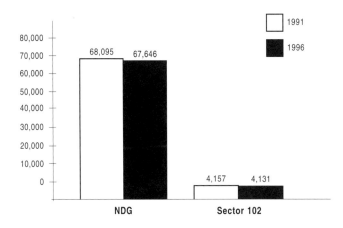

Figure 4.4. Both the overall population of NDG and the population of sector 102 have fallen over a recent five-year period (after CLSC NDG/Montréal-Ouest 2000, and Statistics Canada 1999).

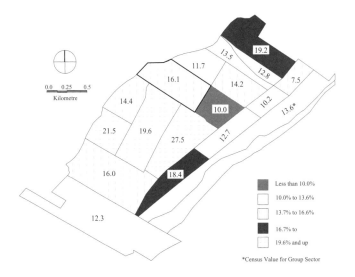

Figure 4.5. The proportion of elderly people within the overall population varies widely within NDG. The sector-by-sector proportion of the elderly population, including sector 102, is shown here (after CLSC NDG/Montréal-Ouest 2000).

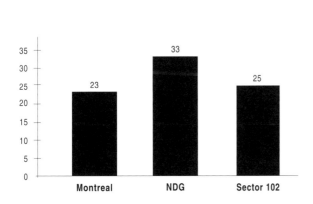

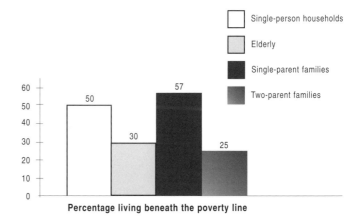

Figure 4.6. One-third of all families in NDG are single-parent families—higher than the proportion for Montreal as a whole (after CLSC NDG/Montréal-Ouest 2000, and Statistics Canada 2000, 1999).

Figure 4.8. The percentages of people of different groups living beneath the poverty line in NDG have all increased over the levels of the preceding five years (after CLSC NDG/Montréal-Ouest 2000).

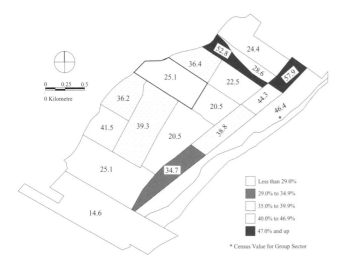

Figure 4.7. More families in NDG are single-parent families than in Montreal as a whole. The sector-by-sector proportion of single-parent families in NDG, including sector 102, is shown here (after CLSC NDG/Montréal-Ouest 2000).

Sector 102 has an extremely high percentage of single-person households compared with NDG (39% versus 18%). This is notable because all housing on the site was designed to accommodate a "typical" North American family with two parents and children. Many of the single-person households in sector 102 consist of elderly people. Of the sector's elderly population, 36% live alone.

The proportion of people living beneath the poverty line increased dramatically in NDG from 1990 (25%) to 1995 (32%). Poverty is a significant problem for many segments of the population living in NDG (Figure 4.8). A factor that has potentially contributed to NDG's rising rate of poor households is its increase in unemployed residents. The percentage grew steadily from 8% in 1981 to 12% in 1996. Of all those in the paid labour force in sector 102, 8% consider their homes to be their regular place of work.

Looking at the above information, many conclusions regarding the needs of the present and likely future demographics of the area can be drawn and addressed. For example, the housing demands in Notre-Dame-de-Grâce in the near future show signs of changing in a way that is particularly relevant to the following planning and simulation. Also, the decreasing household size (because of fewer children or the presence of only one parent) and the increase in elderly and single-person homes will be addressed. The rising percentage of those living in poverty (especially the elderly) or who are unemployed demand intervention through new regulations or social programs in order to maintain the harmony and wholeness of the NDG character. In understanding the dynamics of this particular site, it is possible to augment planning practices and regulations to accommodate the needs of the present and future populations.

The site—sector 102—on which the new suburban modification planning was applied, is bounded on the east by Grand Boulevard, on the south by Somerled Avenue, on the west by Kensington Avenue, and on the north by Fielding Avenue. Figures 4.9 and 4.10 show the site at differing scales within the suburban fabric of NDG. The modified Cape Cod houses of the neighbourhood are laid-out lots that average 15.3 m by 30.5 m (50 ft by 100 ft), with a 7 m (23 ft) setback from the street. Typically, there is at least one full-grown tree in the front yard, and an ample yard in the rear of each home.

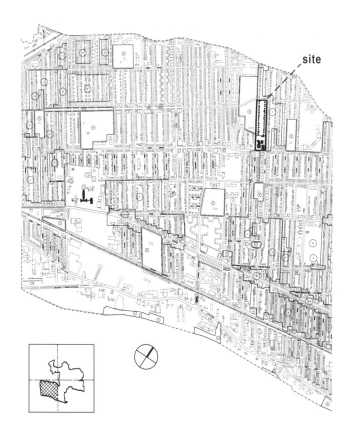

Figure 4.9. The site in sector 102 is located in the northern-central section of the southwest quadrant of the municipality of Notre-Dame-de-Grâce.

Figure 4.11 illustrates the housing and spatial types of the neighbourhood, and gives an indication of their proximity to community facilities.

At the south end of the block, there are two churches, a six-storey apartment building, and a public library that also serves

- ☐ Single family detached units
- ■ Semi-detached & low-rise apartments
- ☐ Public parks
- ☐ Civic building

Figure 4.10. The site in sector 102 is bounded by Somerled Avenue and Fielding Avenue to the south and north, respectively, and by Grand Boulevard and Kensington Avenue to the east and west, respectively. It is adjacent to a playing field to the east and community amenities to the south.

Figure 4.11. The housing on the site is primarily of the detached, single-family type. To the south of the site, however, there are apartments in a low-rise building block.

Figure 4.12. The commercial and institutional neighbourhood context of the study site includes churches, a public library, and shopping on Somerled Avenue. From top: Christ Memorial Church, Fraser Hickson Library, and Somerled Avenue.

as a popular community centre. These buildings are adjacent to Somerled Avenue, which is a busy street lined with various commercial activities serving this neighbourhood as well as a much larger area of NDG (Figure 4.12). Just across Kensington Avenue from the site are a large park, a public swimming pool, and a running track. This park is a popular gathering place for children and adults of the nearby community. There are public bus stops on both Grand Boulevard and Somerled Avenue. Surrounding the site is a primarily residential area. Housing is typically of the semi-detached, low-rise apartment and postwar single-family variety.

The Notre-Dame-de-Grâce district is subject to the municipal control of the City of Montreal. Sector 102 is zoned for use and occupancy as H.1, meaning that only single-family detached units may be built. The site coverage and density of a single unit may not exceed 50%. Though this block was developed during the 1940s, when zero-lot line construction was permitted, today the city prevents this practice with an alignment zoning regulation. All new construction, such as additions, must conform to the city planning regulation U.1, which means that home and professional offices and artist's studios are allowed to exist. Also, zoning limits the height of units to 9 m (30 ft) and/or one storey. A page from the NDG zoning manual corresponding with this regulation is shown in Figure 4.13. Zoning regulation regarding the architectural elements and characteristics of buildings is limited to external applications. The finish of the building is required to be of stone or

Figure 4.13. The existing zoning regulations (summary shown here) ensure that a consistency of design and placement of units in the neighbourhood are maintained; however, strict adherence to the controls as they exist will effectively mummify the neighbourhood.

Building and Lot Size

▶ The building type must be a single-family detached unit.
▶ The average lot size is 15.3 m by 30.5 m (50 ft by 100 ft).
▶ The average unit size is 87.9 m² (945 ft²) or about 8.2 m by 10.7 m (27 ft by 35 ft).

Orientation of the Lot

▶ Lateral lot lines must be perpendicular to the street.
▶ In the case of corner lots, the smallest dimension must address the street.

Width of the Block

▶ The block cannot accommodate more than two rows of lots back to back.

Building Size

▶ The maximum height of buildings is 9 m (29.5 ft) and/or one storey.
▶ Existing units may add a second storey.

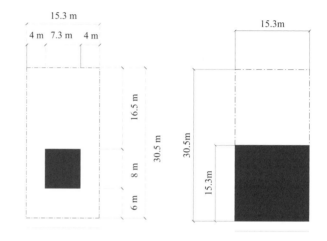

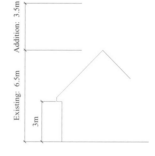
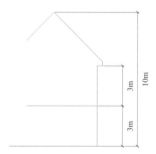

brick, the roof must be pitched in a gable, hip, or mansard, and it must address the street. Also, the percentage of openings per building facade ranges from a minimum of 20% to a maximum of 40%.

The Planning Proposal

The theoretical framework established at the beginning of this chapter and complemented by demographic and legislative information will now be applied to the experimental site in NDG. First, a brief assessment of existing conditions (representing Steps 1 and 2 of the planning process) will be made. Based on this assessment, a vision of the future of the neighbourhood will be presented (Step 3). Next (Step 4), a design concept with a concise list of the objectives to be achieved in order to realize the vision will be developed, which will then be translated into an illustrated site plan (Step 5). This site plan will show a simulated future form of the neighbourhood that could be produced through a combination of communal and individual desires and the application of the new design code (Step 6). The solutions that will be presented are viable ones; it is understood, however, that the concept and code could very easily produce a suburban form that varies from the picture painted in the following experiment, all depending upon the desires and dynamics of the existing neighbourhood.

Notre-Dame-de-Grâce is a well-respected and pleasant neighbourhood of Montreal. Though it contains a variety of household types, it has physically stagnated over the last few decades. The fact that this stagnation has been a gradual one raises the question of why now is the appropriate time to intervene in this neighbourhood. The pressures acting on this quiet community have been steadily building. When the breaking point arrives (when the community is no longer able to support a healthy population and begins a self-propagating cycle of deterioration), it may be too late to enact progressive ideas.

The pressures acting on NDG are not unique. The steady rise in the elderly population of North America is causing communities everywhere to re-evaluate their priorities; in only a few years, when baby boomers begin to retire, communities that have not planned for it may find themselves incapable of supplying the particular housing demands of this enormous market sector. Similarly, the falling birth rates and climbing divorce rates of recent years have created many small households. The suburb unwilling or unable to adapt to such housing demands could conceivably be left with unusable housing stock. Also, the pace of technological change so greatly surpasses the ability of current development and control mechanisms to adapt that suburban communities anchored in past form may similarly become unsuitable places for North Americans to live in. Many communities, much like NDG, need to act before pressures such as these damage the livability of the area.

These pressures raise the issue of what the role of planning is in providing solutions to problems that are apparently social in nature. Constance Perin, in the 1977 publication *Everything in Its Place*, points out that it is impossible to look at housing in isolation, as the type, tenure, and location of a household's residence are a primary determinant of the household's access to other aspects of society, such as education, employment, and community life. Furthermore, and at a more rudimentary level, providing affordable suitable housing frees residents' incomes for other equally important items. It has been well documented that an individual's ability to choose the residence that best suits his or her needs provides an irreplaceable source of self-esteem and fulfillment (Teasdale and Wexler 1993; Becker 1977; Morris and Winter 1975, 1978).

Sector 102 in NDG is an appropriate site for testing an intervention, as it is already beginning to exhibit signs of damage due to unmet needs and can be perceived as a microcosm that is representative of the problems and issues that North American suburbia will soon have to face, such as continued growth of its large population of elderly residents, and with it the problem of finding suitable housing; rising living expenses; and maintaining a social network. Enabling elderly residents to create and abide in accessible, easily maintained housing units in their community, such as ancillary units or "garden suites," is an important response to these issues. Allowing elderly homeowners to subdivide their homes to contain rental units provides another way for them to remain in their home community in housing suited to their needs. Additionally, the high percentage of households experiencing an affordability gap in NDG is an indicator of an emerging community crisis. Many households would benefit from expense-reducing housing options, such as the conversion of a portion of their unit into a home office or rental unit. Furthermore, the divergent housing needs of the numerous single-parent and single-person households in NDG demand a variety of housing and tenure options, such as home sharing and ancillary units. Such augmentations of orthodox housing types are essential to the future health of the NDG community.

The vision for this neighbourhood stems directly from the housing and community needs previously discussed. The percentage of elderly residents, single people, and households with fewer children will continue to grow relative to the total population. Housing costs will rise. Efficiency and ecological and economic concerns will likely move to the forefront of people's concerns. In addition to all this, transportation costs and advances in communications technology through the Internet and the personal computer will further blur the defining line between "at work" and "at home."

It is acknowledged that this community has a definite character and that it is the residents' desire to maintain that character. This is one of the fundamental criteria underlying the neighbourhood vision. The three components of the vision of the neighbourhood's future development are the built environment, the open space, and circulation and parking.

The architectural vocabulary of single-family, postwar homes defines the built character of this neighbourhood. Preserving it is important. The function of the built environment,

Figure 4.14. More accommodating sidewalks can increase community awareness and understanding of changes that may be occurring. Planting provides a certain degree of privacy and lighting security for such rest areas.

Figure 4.15. It is important to provide lanes for bicycles and pedestrian traffic. As the economic and social nature of the suburb becomes more complex, these modes of transportation will be increasingly relied upon.

therefore, must operate within this condition. In response to the great need for unit-type options, the internal subdivision of homes and the construction of ancillary units in the backyards of individual homes would be encouraged. A greater use of home office spaces for small-scale community commercial activities would also be encouraged. Such changes would be introduced on the basis of residents' needs, and physical modifications would occur in the interior and at the rear of existing units. Such subtle changes should enable the neighbourhood to evolve gradually and gracefully.

The impact of increasing community density as a result of these functional changes can be minimized through the careful alteration and articulation of open space. Particular attention should be paid to the issue of public versus private space, since the distinction between public and private becomes less explicit when units' spatial envelopes begin to shrink. Casual interaction between residents becomes important during times of transition since it provides a non-aggressive opportunity to

discuss impending changes, thereby easing fears and increasing community understanding. The NDG neighbourhood under consideration would benefit from an embellishment of the sidewalks or street edges and the provision of small focal points where community members could gather informally. Also, since the neighbourhood benefits today from the presence of fully grown trees, further planting along the street in order to buffer pedestrians and homes from vehicular traffic would be encouraged, as sketched in Figure 4.14.

The proposed development of open space relates closely to the envisioned circulation through the neighbourhood. The possibility that fuel may become prohibitively expensive in the future would change the way North America commutes in suburbia. A greater reliance on public transportation has been considered. Also, the potential for increased bicycle use and greater volume of pedestrian traffic is addressed by the provision of bicycle lanes and pleasant and safe sidewalks along neighbourhood streets, as depicted in Figure 4.15. Despite the

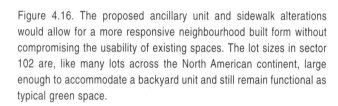

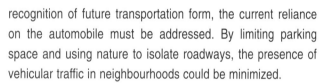

Figure 4.16. The proposed ancillary unit and sidewalk alterations would allow for a more responsive neighbourhood built form without compromising the usability of existing spaces. The lot sizes in sector 102 are, like many lots across the North American continent, large enough to accommodate a backyard unit and still remain functional as typical green space.

Figure 4.17. Modification of the sidewalk in the manner illustrated will both increase the intimacy and human scale of the neighbourhood and decrease the obnoxious effects that vehicular traffic has on pedestrian traffic and home life.

recognition of future transportation form, the current reliance on the automobile must be addressed. By limiting parking space and using nature to isolate roadways, the presence of vehicular traffic in neighbourhoods could be minimized.

Having explored the community's needs and formulated a vision for the site, a structure of objectives can now be laid out. Built upon these objectives will be an overall design concept in the form of a site plan and an augmented design code.

The built structures in the neighbourhood should respond to socio-economic and demographic changes by incorporating light commercial uses and tenure-type alternatives, such as the ancillary units depicted in Figure 4.16.

Modifications and additions made to the existing built structures should not detract from the visual harmony of the community and should respect the neighbours' privacy, rights, and aspirations.

Created at an appropriate scale, the use of various types of home offices by residents should be an asset to community members as well as an affordable and ecologically sound alternative to commuting.

Public spaces should serve as informal community gathering sites and offer places for rest and recreation for adults and children. Sidewalks should be considered public gathering places and should therefore include foliage buffers between pedestrians and the street. Enhancing sidewalks will allow for an increase in pedestrian traffic in the neighbourhood and surrounding areas. Sketches, such as the one illustrating this concept in Figure 4.17, and the previous two, are invaluable in illustrating concepts laid out in the formalizing process. Any future landscaping should respect the presence of mature trees already on the site.

Encouraging pedestrian and bicycle traffic, as well as making public transportation widely accessible and convenient, should reduce the number of cars in use within the community. Vehicular traffic and parking should be addressed in a way that enhances the character of the community and ensures the safety of residents. The perceived presence of traffic and its speed should not increase with any increase in the density of the neighbourhood.

These objectives are expressed in the site plan shown in Figure 4.18, and they are contrasted with the existing site conditions. In Figure 4.19, the previous incremental development of sector 102 is shown in a continuum with projected future development. Though such a site design is hypothetical, such projections—snapshots of the future, really—serve to illustrate the potential effectiveness of the proposed planning process as it would occur in indistinct phases.

Conceiving growth in phases is a critical aspect of the design process for several reasons. First, piecemeal growth emphasizes the fact that a wholesale change is not being

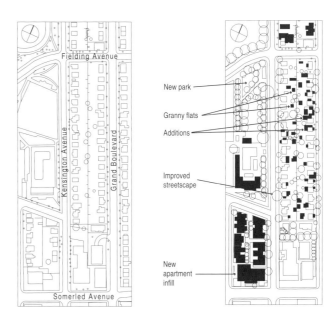

Figure 4.18. The existing site plan (left) is contrasted with one scenario for a more responsive site plan (right). Note that ancillary units were added at the rear of lots and some of the structures have had additions constructed (both shown in black).

imposed upon this community. Instead, the changes are motivated by the needs of individual households. The plan reflects the process's ability to incorporate this individuality into a coherent community image. Second, depicting piecemeal growth reflects the realistic nature of the proposal, as individual unit alterations are likely to be made only as personal resources allow. Third, portraying the process as it would occur over a period of many years acknowledges the somewhat cyclical nature of household changes: families begin as a couple, grow as children arrive, shrink as children leave home, and may then

1945-1955	1955-1970	1970-2000	2000-2010	2010-2030
Agricultural land is converted to residential use as the need to house new immigrants increases. Single-family detached houses 80 m² (800 ft²) in size are constructed. The surrounding roads are not yet paved. There are few civic buildings. Transportation to the area is light.	*In 1960, the Fraser Hickson Library moves to its location on the southwest corner of the study block. A church is located on the southeast corner. More homes are constructed in the adjacent blocks. A process of alteration begins in some of the homes.*	*An apartment block is built on the southeast corner of the block. A modern expansion to the church is constructed next door. More additions and interior alterations take place in the homes.*	*As a result of mounting pressures and demographic changes, the City of Montreal introduces new bylaws that permit the construction of ancillary units as well as additions or the partition of a dwelling unit into two. Some residents act swiftly on the changes and build additions.*	*A process of accretion continues: more homeowners make additions and renovations. The community experiences gentrification. The lower-level dwelling units of the apartment block on the southeast corner are converted to shops.*

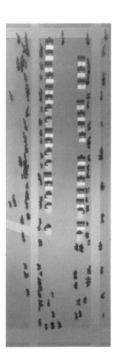 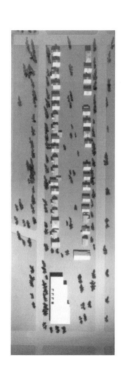 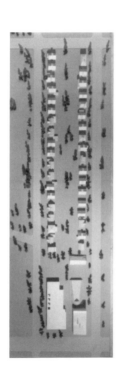 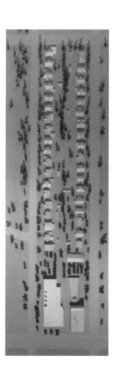 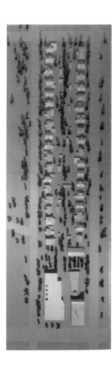

Figure 4.19. The models show aerial images of the evolution of the simulation block from the time of its construction during the 1940s until the year 2030.

be only a single-member household in old age. Finally, other changes, not obvious from the site plan (ones that occur within the units, for example), should be considered. These functional and physical unit changes are considered in greater detail below.

It is also important to note that the site plan includes macro-level changes made to the block, such as rest areas and planting along the street edge. Such changes would require the intervention of the municipality. It has been included in the plan in order to encourage the possibility of these improvements.

The design code for sector 102 of Notre-Dame-de-Grâce is based upon the steps that have preceded it, and hopefully is applicable to a wider area than just this neighbourhood.

An important component of the proposal is the introduction of ancillary units (also known as garden suites or granny flats). These units have already been added on a limited basis to other neighbourhoods across North America and provide a solution to a wide range of affordable housing needs. The floor plan of a demonstration garden suite sponsored by Canada Mortgage and Housing Corporation (CMHC) is shown in Figure 4.20.

While ancillary units would be beneficial to NDG as rental units for single-person or elderly households, or possibly as small-scale professional offices, their appearance and perceived presence must be regulated in order to ensure their acceptability to residents. The proposed design code requires that ancillary units be located entirely behind the original house,

Bird's-eye view of proposed garden suites in study site

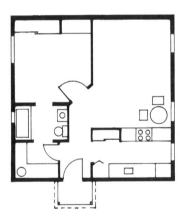

CMHC garden suite floor plan

Figure 4.20. In a 1994 publication entitled *Designs Produced for the Demonstration and Other Installations of Garden Suites*, Canada Mortgage and Housing Corporation designed a garden suite meant to be applied in the same manner as proposed in this figure. The difference, however, is that, due to private concerns in sector 102, ancillary units will be personalized to a much greater degree.

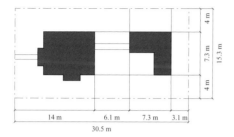

Figure 4.21. The lot plan for an ancillary unit addition will ensure that the character of the neighbourhood is not injured by an overbearing addition. Mandatory setbacks and alignments in relation to the original unit would be instituted.

Figure 4.22. Height limitations in relation to the original unit would also ensure a certain subordination of the ancillary unit to the existing one.

so that it would not conflict with the neighbourhood's existing character and the vision of future development. An example that would conform to such restrictions is illustrated in Figure 4.21. Setbacks intended to preserve the privacy of unit occupants and neighbours are also indicated. Restricting the location of porches and prohibiting windows in the rear facade of ancillary units also preserves privacy.

The size of the new structure should also guarantee its subordination to the existing home. As seen in Figure 4.22, backyard units' heights would be restricted, and it follows that so would the scale of any commercial activity that could be located in the units.

Ancillary units could be either prefabricated or built with a permanent basement, depending upon the desires and resources of the residents of the existing unit. The new units would be owned and maintained by the owner of the main house on the property. In this way, garden suites could provide the method by which postwar suburbia can meet the growing alternative housing needs of North America.

The new design code, based on the particularities of the NDG site, is laid out in Figure 4.23, which contains a more elaborate consideration of ancillary unit design.

The proposed planning focuses on the evolution of existing neighbourhoods where the infrastructure is already complete, the surrounding areas have an established functional pattern, and the residents have a clear perception of the character of their community. In such a neighbourhood, it has been stipulated that growth would occur primarily through changes to individual homes. Since residents will make these unit-based decisions themselves, the process allows for much less control than is afforded to planners of totally new developments. And since such changes are made on a small scale, planning interventions must be highly sensitive.

Figure 4.23. A possible design code, specific to the NDG site, has been developed. By taking steps similar to those in the existing code, neighbourhood continuity and harmony are maintained. New construction would be accommodated, however, and further economic and social development of the neighbourhood would be fostered.

Circulation

▶ On-street parking:

  • Street width over 15 m   parking on both sides

  • 7-15 m   parking on one side

  • 4-7 m   parking on one side

  • under 4 m   no parking

▶ A 1 m wide bicycle lane shall be designated along all through streets.

▶ A minimum of one and a maximum of two on-site space(s) shall be provided per dwelling unit.

▶ Driveways shall have a hard surface.

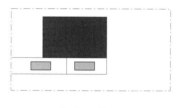

On-site parking

The Built Environment

Architectural Elements

▶ All structures shall be clad with wood, brick, stone, or reproductions of these materials made from recycled materials.

▶ Brick mortar joints shall be struck.

▶ New or replacement windows and doors shall be of a material which matches or simulates the existing material and is compatible with the design of the existing primary unit (energy-efficient windows and doors are recommended).

▶ Facades shall have between 20% and 40% glazed openings.

▶ All roof slopes shall be between 4:12 and 8:12.

▶ All roofs shall be clad with asphalt or similar products made of recycled material.

▶ Roofs of bay windows, porches, and similar extensions may be of galvanized material.

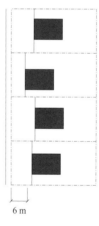

6 m

Front projection alignment

Additions

▶ Front setbacks shall be at least 6 m from the front property line or aligned with the furthest projection on the block.

▶ Side setbacks shall be at least 1.5 m from side property lines.

▶ Rear setback shall be at least 10 m from rear property line.

▶ Front additions shall be no larger than 1.5 m x 50% of the length of the unit, or 5 m x 50% of the length of the unit if the stairs are included.

Figure 4.23 continued

▸ Front additions shall have gable or hip roofs.

▸ Architectural elements guidelines (presented above) apply.

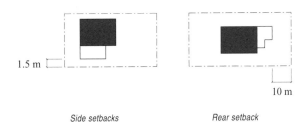

1.5 m

10 m

Side setbacks   *Rear setback*

Unit Subdivision

▸ A rental apartment unit is permitted within the existing unit.

▸ Apartment unit size shall be between 30 and 50 m².

max. area: 30-50 m²

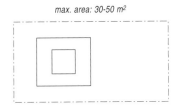

Additional apartment area as a percentage of existing unit area

Home Offices

▸ No more than 1/3 of the existing unit area to a maximum of 50 m² may be used for commercial purposes within a primary unit.

▸ Home office uses must not interfere with the residential nature of the neighbourhood and therefore should be of light commercial use.

▸ Acceptable uses may include home offices, child care, and professional services.

▸ Home office spaces are intended for the use of the residents of the home only.

▸ No illuminated or free-standing signs are permitted to advertise the home business; no sign may exceed 0.5 m.

max. area: 30-50 m²

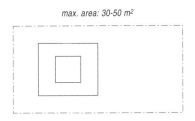

Home office area as a percentage of existing unit area

Ancillary Units

▸ May be placed/constructed in the backyard of any existing unit.

▸ May not be built higher than one storey or 4.9 m.

▸ Maximum unit area is 50 m².

▸ Shall be located within the width of the existing primary unit, and placed at least 6 m from the rear facade of the existing primary unit.

▸ Shall be placed at least 3 m from the rear property line.

▸ A mezzanine is permitted within the unit.

▸ No openings are permitted within the rear facade.

▸ May be attached to the primary unit using a walkway.

▸ Any porches, decks, or terraces:

  • shall be on the facade that faces the primary unit

  • shall be no longer than 1.8 m x 50% of the unit length

  • shall be made from natural materials or simulated natural material made of recycled elements

Figure 4.23 continued

▶ Architectural Elements guidelines apply with the following changes:

    • Roof material may also be wood shingles or shakes.

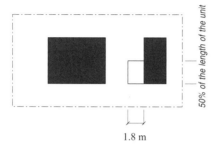

Size and location of porches and decks of ancillary unit

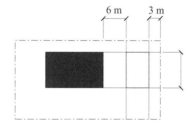

Placement of ancillary unit

Corner Lots

▶ Front setback shall be 7 m from front property line.

▶ Rear setback shall be 8 m from rear property line.

▶ Side setback shall be 1.5 m from side property lines.

▶ No ancillary units are permitted.

▶ Building height shall not exceed two storeys or 10 m.

▶ Architecture Elements guidelines apply.

▶ Home office guidelines apply with the following changes:

    • No more than 50% of the unit may be used for light commercial activities.

    • Acceptable uses may also include dépanneur/convenience store, café, or hairdresser.

    • No illuminated signs are permitted to advertise the home business; no sign may exceed 1 m².

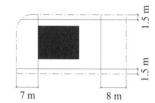

Corner lot unit setbacks

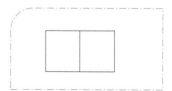

Corner lot commercial space as a percentage of existing unit

Figure 4.23 continued

Garages

▶ Maximum height: 3.8 m.

▶ Maximum area: 32.5 m^2

▶ Maximum size opening per wall surface shall be 1.5 m^2 (excluding garage door[s]).

▶ No underground parking.

▶ Architectural Elements guidelines apply with the following changes:

   • Roof may be flat.

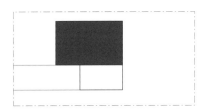

Garage size limit

Front Porches

▶ Maximum area: 1.5 m x 50% of the length of the unit, or 5 m x 50% of the length of the unit if the stairs are included.

▶ Shall be constructed of natural materials or reproductions made of recycled materials.

▶ Porches may have gable or hip roofs, or a shed roof sloping away from the house facade.

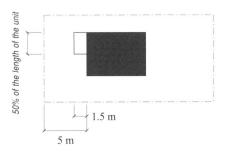

Front porch size limit

Back Porches and Decks

▶ Shall not cover more than 1/3 of rear yard or extend more than 4.5 m from the unit.

▶ Shall not extend more than 1 m beyond the side of the unit.

▶ Deck floor shall not be higher than the existing interior floor line.

▶ Shall be constructed of natural materials or reproductions made of recycled materials; the structure shall be constructed of wood and/or concrete.

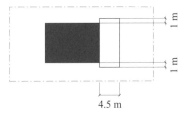

Back porch size limits

Figure 4.23 continued

Public Space and Landscape

▸ A landscaped buffer of at least 1 m wide should be installed between all sidewalks and the street.

▸ Sidewalks should be at least 1 m in width; wider sidewalks are encouraged.

▸ All pedestrian crossings should be signified on the street with paint or a different surfacing material.

▸ All sidewalks and public paths should be lit by lamps no more than 15 m apart.

▸ Trees indigenous to the area should be planted where they are needed to achieve 10 m between trees along the street.

▸ Rest areas for pedestrians should be placed at intersections, in the middle of long blocks, and at bus stops; no more than two rest areas suggested per intersection.

▸ Rest areas should offer places to sit, and be lit and landscaped.

▸ All trees planted in public areas, along sidewalks, and near rest areas shall be nursery-grown and at least 5 m in height when planted.

▸ Public spaces should be furnished with one trash can per 50 m² area.

▸ Public spaces should be covered with at least 2/3 vegetation, and provide at least one bench per 20 m².

▸ Individual lots should be covered by at least 20% vegetation (excluding the area of the unit and any additional structures).

▸ All landscaping should respect the views from the neighbouring properties, as well as the views to and from the street, porches, and public spaces.

▸ Fences or natural barriers should be constructed of natural materials only and shall not exceed 2 m in height; front perimeter fences shall not exceed 0.9 m in height.

▸ Swimming pools are not permitted.

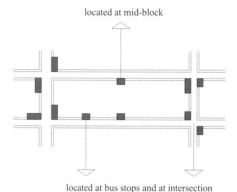

Location of rest areas

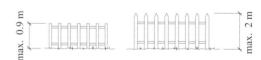

Fence and natural barrier height limits

The ability to upgrade the function of the house by adding or changing the use of rooms is desirable for various reasons. Making this change is considerably less expensive and disruptive than moving, and the psychological importance of modifying the house to suit owners' needs cannot be underestimated. The process of assessing needs and then taking steps to satisfy them is a basic human response that leads to a greater sense of self-esteem and well-being. The possibility of altering the home is one of the most fundamental advantages of homeownership.

As previously discussed, the pace of change in contemporary society has rendered obsolete the postwar house, designed around the single earner and the nuclear, car-dependent family. However, the modified Cape Cod home model used in Notre-Dame-de-Grâce and across North America as well as other postwar home designs often carry within their generic frames the ability to change with the times. Many postwar homes were deliberately designed to be expanded and changed when the household had the need and resources to do so (Friedman 1995). The postwar Flexabilt Home, as seen in *House and Home Magazine* in 1952, is an example of a housing design that adapts to family dynamics. One possible change cycle of this home is depicted in Figure 4.24.

In addition to being important on a personal level, enabling and encouraging individuals to make changes to their homes in the proposed manner can be beneficial to municipalities (Schlaepfer 1983). For example, while addressing the need to rehabilitate existing housing stock, there is an opportunity to create additional housing units that would benefit the community as a whole. Also, rather than extending suburban fabric, existing infrastructure is used more thoroughly with the proposed increase in density. And the approval of higher densities in older areas could provide developers with an economic incentive to revitalize them. Finally, allowing commercial and rental subdivision of existing units raises the tax base of the municipality without requiring a significant augmentation of services.

Housing alterations as considered in the proposed planning process can be described in three broad categories: use modification, internal physical alteration, and external physical alteration (Schlaepfer 1983). These categories are elaborated on diagramatically in Figures 4.25 and 4.26. Within the categories, an almost infinite number of scenarios are possible.

Pantelopoulos, in her 1993 thesis entitled "Small Living Spaces: A Study of Space Management in Wartime Homes in Montreal," conducted a study of modifications made to postwar houses in Montreal suburbs. Through a series of questionnaires, interviews, and site visits, she recorded an inventory of the alterations that had been performed. These alterations were documented on floor plans, an example of which is seen in Figure 4.27.

Several broad trends can be found in the results of her study. First, the kitchen is the area that is the focus of most of

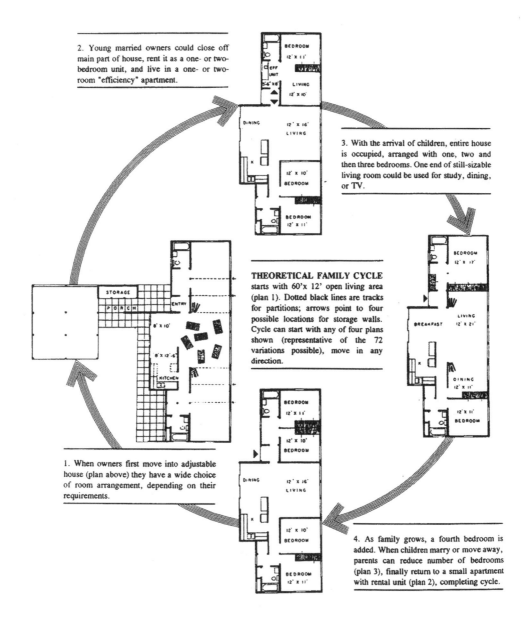

2. Young married owners could close off main part of house, rent it as a one- or two-bedroom unit, and live in a one- or two-room "efficiency" apartment.

3. With the arrival of children, entire house is occupied, arranged with one, two and then three bedrooms. One end of still-sizable living room could be used for study, dining, or TV.

THEORETICAL FAMILY CYCLE starts with 60'x 12' open living area (plan 1). Dotted black lines are tracks for partitions; arrows point to four possible locations for storage walls. Cycle can start with any of four plans shown (representative of the 72 variations possible), move in any direction.

1. When owners first move into adjustable house (plan above) they have a wide choice of room arrangement, depending on their requirements.

4. As family grows, a fourth bedroom is added. When children marry or move away, parents can reduce number of bedrooms (plan 3), finally return to a small apartment with rental unit (plan 2), completing cycle.

Figure 4.24. The Flexabilt Home was intended to change with the dynamics of North American family life. The Cape Cod homes of NDG are similarly able to change gracefully with the passing of time and changing of social conditions (*House and Home* 1952).

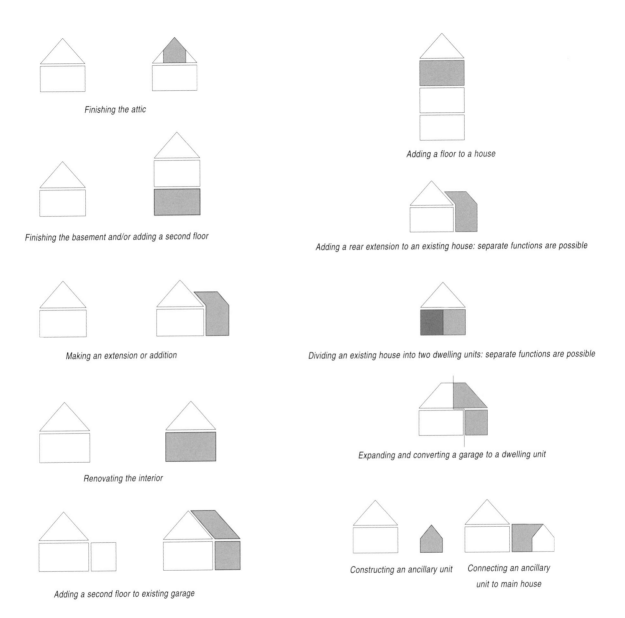

Finishing the attic

Finishing the basement and/or adding a second floor

Making an extension or addition

Renovating the interior

Adding a second floor to existing garage

Adding a floor to a house

Adding a rear extension to an existing house: separate functions are possible

Dividing an existing house into two dwelling units: separate functions are possible

Expanding and converting a garage to a dwelling unit

Constructing an ancillary unit   Connecting an ancillary unit to main house

Figure 4.25. The range of alteration possibilities under the existing design code.

Figure 4.26. The possibilities of mixed uses and multiple dwellings, in contrast with the fairly limiting controls of the existing code, are present in the new design code. A more diverse neighbourhood will result.

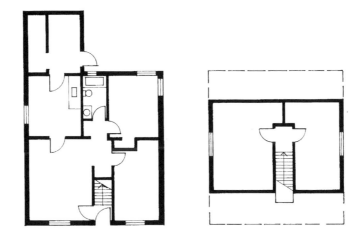

Original plan: ground floor (left), upper floor (right)

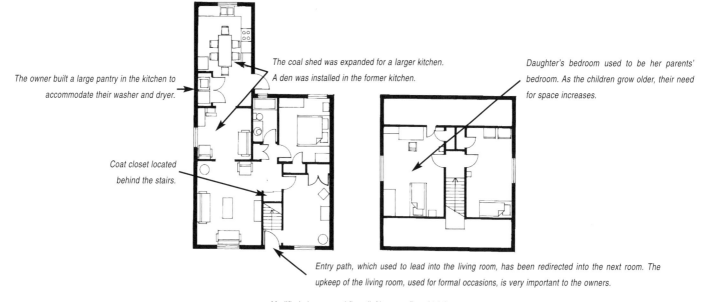

The owner built a large pantry in the kitchen to accommodate their washer and dryer.

The coal shed was expanded for a larger kitchen. A den was installed in the former kitchen.

Daughter's bedroom used to be her parents' bedroom. As the children grow older, their need for space increases.

Coat closet located behind the stairs.

Entry path, which used to lead into the living room, has been redirected into the next room. The upkeep of the living room, used for formal occasions, is very important to the owners.

Modified plan: ground floor (left), upper floor (right)

Figure 4.27. Alterations made to small suburban homes were documented on floor plans of existing units. It is worth noting that the intention of most of the changes was to save space and expand the building envelope (after Pantelopoulos 1993).

the alterations, followed by the children's bedroom. Households generally try to make the kitchen a more open, multi-functional space, as well as to increase the storage capacity of the room. Children's bedrooms have been recognized as areas used not only for sleeping but also as a private space for play and study and as a social space. Few of the documented houses had been given a second bathroom, though most residents felt it would be an added convenience.

Storage was found to be a major problem for occupants of postwar homes, especially in homes with no basement. Residents attempted to utilize unused space in the home, such as the under-stair cavity, for storage. And the lack of storage is further aggravated when original storage space, such as coal sheds or attics, are incorporated into the usable floor area of the house during renovation.

Not surprisingly, elderly residents tended to be much happier living in one-storey homes. Pantelopoulos (1993) points out a key difference between postwar small homes and those built later: because land was a cheap commodity during the postwar boom, homes were built on much larger lots. These larger lots can accommodate later expansions of the home when necessary. Small homes today are invariably built on very small lots, thereby limiting the future adaptability of these homes. For this reason, older suburban developments are the focus of the proposed planning.

Finally, and perhaps most significantly for the purpose of the new planning, Pantelopoulos found that 85% of the residents interviewed felt satisfied with their homes. This indicates, she argued, a willingness to make necessary modifications in a small house in exchange for homeownership.

The houses at the NDG study site are identical to the type studied in Pantelopoulos's study. It is assumed, therefore, that the internal modifications carried out there should follow the same patterns as outlined in the study, though the easily observable, external modifications to the homes in NDG follow other patterns as well. Several actual changes have been recorded in the photographs in Figure 4.28. Many households have enclosed the front porch, creating an informal vestibule and airlock. Few other changes to the front of houses can be observed, however, which contributes to the strong visual character of the community. Many houses have added decks in the rear, and a few have built enclosed back porches. A minority of households have built fully enclosed additions onto the rear or sides of their homes, probably because it is cheaper to make internal space-saving alterations. In a study of small-home adaptations, Rios (1995) reported that the basement is the most multi-functional space in the home. In nearly every case documented that had a basement, the basement had been finished and used in a wide variety of ways. The homes in NDG were constructed with unfinished basements and their subsequent renovation and use probably explain why there are so few exterior additions. Flexible interior design and available outdoor space make even the small uniform houses of the postwar era adaptable and easily personalized.

Figure 4.28. Alterations to existing homes in NDG are typically made only to the interior. In a few homes, pictured here, exterior additions or enclosed porches have been built.

Figure 4.29. The emphasis that the proposed code places on architectural elements, such as building materials and built form, would prevent new construction contrary to the existing character of the neighbourhood and greater NDG. Two examples of construction that is out of character, following the letter but not the intent of current codes, are shown here.

The key to the longevity of a mature suburban neigh-bourhood such as NDG lies in the ability of residents to make necessary modifications to houses. The proposed planning and design code is an effort to guide change so that it can be made with a sensitivity towards the existing community character. Inside the site in NDG, there are instances where changes have been made, within the established control mechanisms of the municipality, that were so radical that the final form of the treated houses were eyesores and did not fit the character of the neighbourhood. The proposed code would work within the established regulations to prevent such oddities, a few of which are shown in Figure 4.29, from occurring in the future.

To illustrate how the new design code would guide neigh-bourhood transformations, six fictional scenarios have been created (see following pages) in which residents of various homes in sector 102 could alter their homes to meet the demands of a changing household. Each scenario is accom-panied by a possible design solution, guided by the proposed new planning code.

Scenario 1: Internal Modification

Occupants: A couple in their mid-fifties.

Event: Their 21-year-old son has returned home after graduating from university ("boomerang" child).

Requirements: The graduate wanted to transform the garage into a studio apartment. The design included a small kitchen, a full bathroom, and a common living/dining/sleeping room. When he is able to find work and live on his own, his parents may want to rent out the apartment to provide additional income. Since construction was going to be done on site, the parents also decided to renovate the interior of the residence.

Existing House: The main house is located mid-block on Kensington Avenue. It has a garage (which is being renovated) and is one of only three houses on the block to have a light stone facade, as opposed to red brick. The front and rear yards are well landscaped with mature trees, shrubs, and floral planting. In the interior of the house, the living room and master bedroom face the park. The kitchen, bathroom, and second bedroom face the backyard. The second floor is accessible though not finished.

Modification: The alteration of the 5 m (16.5 ft) wide garage was done on a low budget. The walls needed only to be insulated, and the opening for the garage filled by a door and windows. Two small windows, one in the bathroom and one in the kitchen, were added to the south facade of the garage apartment, and a sliding door was added leading to the deck in the rear. The interior was left as open space, with the exception of partitioning for the bathroom. Further partitions can be installed to close off a bedroom. As the family renovated the kitchen of the main house, the 2.2 m (7 ft) long original counter, sink, and cabinets were installed in the garage. The only physical link between the existing house and the apartment is the rear deck. This provides privacy for the son and potential tenants, yet allows for contact between the parents and their child.

In addition to the kitchen getting a facelift, the rear bedroom of the existing home was transformed into a den/television room with direct access to the deck. Furthermore, the front of the house was modified by shortening the driveway to allow for landscaping in front of the apartment. The complete before-and-after floor plans, including landscaping, are illustrated in Figure 4.30.

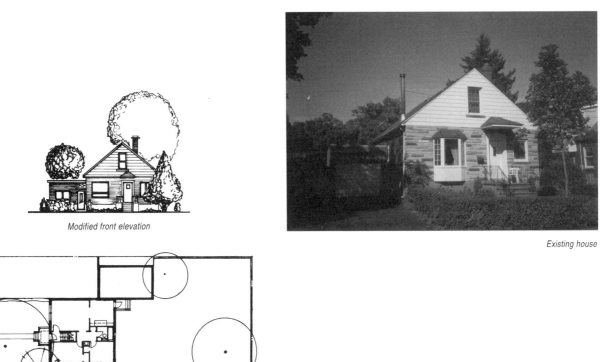

Modified front elevation

Existing house

Existing ground floor

Modified ground floor

Figure 4.30. Scenario 1: The renovation of a unit and its existing garage was required to accommodate a recently graduated university student and his baby-boomer parents. When the young man finally leaves the unit, it can serve the community as alternative housing for students, single people, or the elderly.

Scenario 2: Internal Modification

Occupants: A single father with two teenage children.

Event: The man has remarried. His new wife has a four-year-old boy and the newly formed family, realizing that the house was now too small, decided to renovate the interior.

Requirements: The children wanted separate bedrooms and the teenagers needed a shared bathroom. The newlyweds also wished to have their own master bathroom.

Existing House: The unit is located near the centre of the block along Grand Boulevard. A covered front porch and new fenestration are the only modifications that have been made to the original house. Small trees, shrubs, flower beds, and a wooden fence are the landscaping on site. The interior of the home is still laid out in its original form. The living room and one bedroom are at the front of the house, and the kitchen/dining room and second bedroom are at the rear of the house. A bathroom and staircase are located centrally. The second floor is used for storage, and is divided into two spaces.

Modification: In order to accommodate a family with three children, the storage space of the second floor was turned into a master bedroom and a bedroom for the youngest child. A second bathroom and additional dormer window were also added to the second floor. Only minor door-placement changes were required to ensure privacy on the ground floor for the teenagers. Finally, more cabinets were added to the kitchen, as larger families require more storage space.

Figure 4.31 illustrates the internal renovations that allow a larger family to maintain residence in their original postwar suburban home.

Existing house

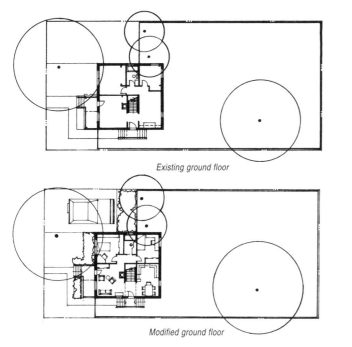

Existing ground floor

Modified ground floor

Existing second floor

Modified second floor

Figure 4.31. Scenario 2: The second floor of an existing unit was required to meet the needs of a growing household. Interior renovations such as this are generally the best way to expand the building envelope and keep costs low.

Scenario 3: Extension to the Home

Occupants: A single mother in her mid-thirties and her seven-year-old daughter.

Event: The woman decided to work at home. She opened her own beauty salon.

Requirements: The salon is located in an addition, and also occupies a small portion of the original floor plan. The daughter's bedroom had to be relocated, and a new bedroom and workspace were designed for the mother.

Existing House: Located at the corner of Fielding Avenue and Kensington Avenue, this house has undergone several previous modifications. A screened porch was added to the rear, the front porch was enclosed (forming a vestibule/airlock), and the brick chimney was replaced by a stainless steel one. Three attractive, mature trees are located on the plot, as well as a hedge that runs around the periphery of the property. The bedrooms, bathroom, kitchen/dining room, and living room are located on the ground floor. The second floor is divided into two spaces—one is used for storage and one is a recreation room.

Modification: An addition to the north and east of the house was planned. Also, the second bedroom was transformed into part of the beauty salon. The entrance to the salon is on Fielding Avenue, while the front door of the house remains on Kensington Avenue. The first-floor bathroom is the link between the house and salon, and is used by both. The exterior brick walls on the northeast corner of the house were removed, except for a column and two beams supporting the roof. The mother's bedroom has been moved to the second floor, where a small office is now adjacent to it. There is now a family room on the second floor.

Figure 4.32 shows the original and combination residential/commercial ground-floor plans.

Modified side elevation

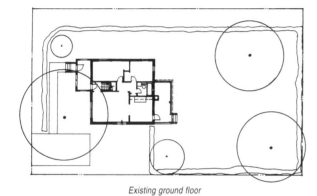

Existing ground floor

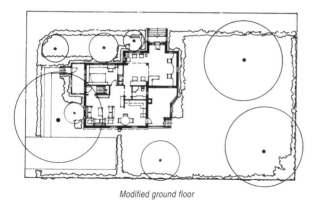

Modified ground floor

Figure 4.32. Scenario 3: To accommodate the opening of a neighbourhood business, a beauty salon, an addition was made to an existing unit on the corner of Fielding Avenue and Kensington Avenue. In addition, the second floor was developed as a home office and recreation room.

Scenario 4: Extension to the House

Occupants: A young couple about to have their first child.

Event: In order to meet a community need and work conveniently while taking care of a newborn, the couple decided to open a desktop publishing service in the home.

Requirements: The office required a separate entrance and the interior of the house had to be renovated. Also, a portion of the backyard had to be designed as a play area for the expected child.

Existing House: This unit is adjacent to the Scenario 2 home, and is its mirror image. The landscaping includes a flower bed in the front yard and two mature trees in the rear. There are various shrubs on the lot as well. The interior arrangements on the ground floor are identical to the neighbouring house, and the second floor is separated into two spaces and used only for storage.

Modification: A 35 m^2 (350 ft^2) addition has been built on the northwest corner of the home. It contains the publishing office. The main office entrance faces Grand Boulevard. A path from the sidewalk leads up to it.

In the interior of the house, a new powder room and a small kitchen have been built in the area where the rear bedroom was located. The existing door of the bedroom serves as the threshold between the office and home. A sliding door on the north facade gives access to a raised wooden deck from the kitchen. The remainder of the house has been redesigned with an open plan. Living and dining rooms are located at the front of the unit; sleeping quarters for parents and child, along with a new bathroom, have been relocated to the second floor.

The original unit and redesign are illustrated in Figure 4.33.

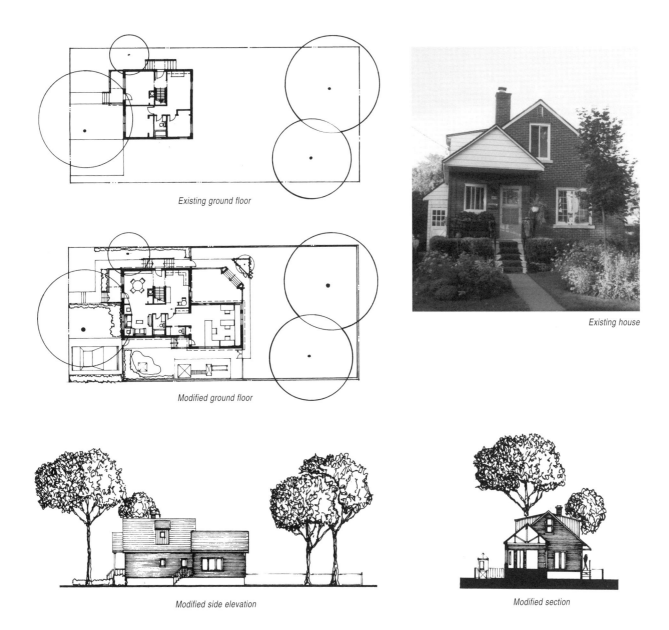

Existing ground floor

Modified ground floor

Existing house

Modified side elevation

Modified section

Figure 4.33. Scenario 4: The creation of another local business, a desktop publishing office, required an addition to the rear of a unit. A separate entrance was needed, and the space of the existing unit was reorganized. A new recreational space—a raised wooden deck—was added.

Scenario 5: New Building

Occupants: A couple in their early forties, with two teenagers.

Event: An aging parent, in her late sixties, has moved in with the family.

Requirements: A garden suite with a walkway connected to the main house was desired. This should allow the family both privacy and convenience. The garden suite can later be used as a rental unit.

Existing House: The house is on the southwest corner of the residential area along Kensington Avenue. A paved one-car driveway is located at the south of the lot, and little formal landscaping has been attempted. A small, covered wooden front porch has been added. The existing floor plan is standard, with two bedrooms, a small bathroom, and a kitchen/dining room. The second floor is used for storage.

Modification: The 44 m^2 (440 ft^2) garden suite is located behind the existing house, and a covered walkway connects the two. It is raised a few feet off the ground but is accessible via a ramp that is part of the walkway. Even though it may be necessary for the elderly parent to use a wheelchair, it is important that she maintain her independence as long as possible. The interior of the garden suite has a living room and kitchen/dining room facing the original unit, while the bedroom and bathroom are in the rear, to the east.

The relationship of the new unit to the existing one is shown in plan and section in Figure 4.34.

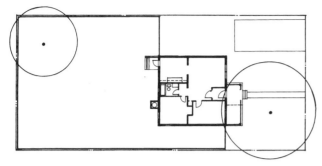

Existing ground floor

Existing house

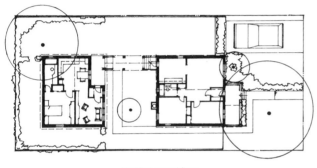

Modified ground floor

Modified site section

New ancillary unit

Figure 4.34. Scenario 5: In a scenario that will become more common in the near future, an aging but independent parent moves in with her middle-aged son and his family. An autonomous garden suite is desired, so that the lifestyles of everyone involved can continue in as normal a fashion as possible.

Scenario 6: New Building

Occupants: A dual-career couple with a five-year-old child.

Event: The wife had recently been laid off and wanted to open her own design office in the home.

Requirements: The wife wanted the design office to be located in an ancillary unit behind the existing house. As her business expands, she expects to hire further personnel, so space was allotted for future growth.

Existing House: Situated near the southeast corner of Grand Boulevard and Somerled Avenue, this unit has undergone several modifications. A one-car garage has been built onto the north side of the unit; an awning has been added over the front entrance; a covered wooden deck, several feet off the ground, has been added at the rear of the house. The backyard has been landscaped with shrubs and flower beds, and contains one mature tree. The interior layout varies from the houses in previous scenarios in that the two bedrooms are located at the front of the ground floor and the kitchen/dining room and living room look onto the backyard.

Modification: The added office, which is about 33 m² (330 ft²) in area, is located in the southeast portion of the rear yard, directly behind the existing unit. The only physical link between the house and the ancillary unit is an open walkway, and the office contains all required facilities. A long path from the sidewalk leads clients past the southern facade of the main house into the backyard to the entrance of the office, which faces southwest. Because the owners of the home use the garage, clients are expected to park in the existing driveway.

Layout changes and the floor plan of the new unit are illustrated in Figure 4.35.

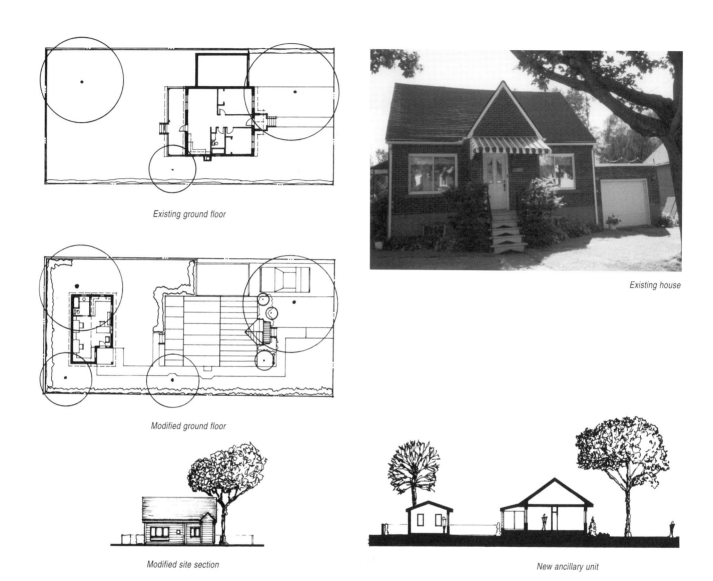

Existing ground floor

Existing house

Modified ground floor

Modified site section

New ancillary unit

Figure 4.35. Scenario 6: In the rear yard, a structure separate from the existing unit was required to house a new design office. With the advent of more sophisticated communications technologies, this is an option that many new businesses may choose, as expenses will be low and business can be conducted with ease outside an urban centre.

This new planning process has been proposed as a direct response to the documented demographic, social, economic, and ecological pressures acting upon suburbia in North America. These pressures will surely worsen in the twenty-first century, and if not addressed may render the suburbs obsolete as a form of settlement. Postwar homes were designed with a remarkable level of ingenuity that enables them to adapt continuously to the changing needs of their occupants, if allowed to. Demands unforeseen by designers a half-century ago, however—such as the task of housing an increasingly elderly population, the escalating costs of natural resources, and the freedoms and idiosyncrasies associated with the Internet and with communications technology—have strained these small homes to their limits. Suburbia itself is trapped in a web of its own developmental regulations and has become part of the problem of housing the North American population, rather than its solution.

Nonetheless, the existing suburbs are not a mistake—they are an opportunity. Mature suburban communities typically offer a high quality of life, though outside pressures have begun to threaten the livability of these areas. Instead of attempting to insulate them from these pressures, adopting a planning procedure that will embrace and guide the future growth of these communities in such a way that their characters are preserved is the answer. Though this concept may not be welcomed in communities that regularly use legislation to curb change, because such a planning procedure is both gradual and resident-initiated, it can be accepted at the pace of a particular community. Gradual and small-scale changes are proposed and regulated by the process, rather than invasive and restrictive ones, in the hope that it will lead the community towards a collectively envisioned future. The new planning process is an acknowledgment that change in these communities is inevitable, and it is an assertion that these changes can be positive ones.

In designing and developing a new suburban fabric, it is important to understand the principle of hierarchical characterization. Such characterization of a system's individual components occurs in practically all areas of study—from linguistics to cosmology to microbiology—where relationships between component parts of a whole can be studied and analyzed to increase understanding of the workings of that system. Understanding of this fundamental hierarchical composition has been important to architectural discussion since the time of the ancients. Moreover, the notion of elemental consecutive significance in the composition of an object (that of a large centre made up of smaller centres, in turn made up of smaller centres, as seen in Figure 5.1)—whether biological, architectural, or artistic—is not a new one. With a hierarchical structure, order can be mapped out, ranking all elements from most influential to least influential. The analytical methodology used can contribute greatly to the understanding of an otherwise incomprehensibly complex unit, such as a city or a suburb. Considering the process of creating new urban outgrowth with an understanding of this principle, it is evident that the current methods of development are insufficient to meet the needs of suburbia at the beginning of the twenty-first century.

Hierarchies of cities and suburbs can take different forms. A traditional version of a city hierarchy may be delineated as follows. The city's downtown is considered the city's most influential element. A city centre has the highest land values, which is indicative of its accessibility to a large number of people and of its activity in the financial and leisure life of the city. Land adjacent to this centre will have its function dictated, to a great extent, by its relationship to the centre. Nearby neighbourhoods may be residential, housing workers of the central business district, or industrial, if close proximity to management

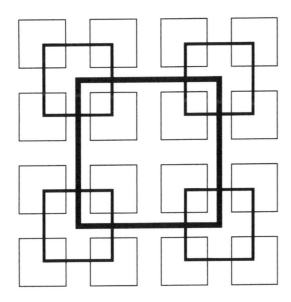

Figure 5.1. Schematically, a whole can be considered to be a pattern of centres composed of smaller centres, whether at a subatomic level or at the scale of a city.

offices is required for such industry. Additionally, each use will be defined by the character of its own centre and the centres of the neighbourhoods that comprise this larger area.

In a residential suburb, the centre of activity may be a high school, a prominent church, or a recreational centre. The suburb may be further broken down into neighbourhoods that may be defined by a corner store or a playground. The neighbourhoods could be broken down into smaller units defined by sidewalk rest areas or cul-de-sacs. Such a breakdown could continue until each fragment of a larger whole is defined by an individual's home. A traditional version of suburban design can consist of several hierarchies: the street (expressway, arterial, collector, local), shopping (regional, community, neighbour-

hood centre), education (college, high school, junior high, elementary), parks (regional, community, neighbourhood, playground), and residential (apartment block, rowhouses, semi-detached homes, single-family homes). Traditional breakdowns such as these can be seen to be collapsing due to various, relatively recent forces: shopping centres (big-box superstores challenge community centres), huge schools (due to lower household size and increased housing density, the elementary school population is frequently not within walking distance, so students must be bused) and multiple school boards (private/public, different languages and religions), street patterns (web versus grid model), and housing patterns (mixed use and various housing types).

How, then, does the theory of hierarchical characterization (in whatever form of hierarchy is chosen) apply to the subject of this chapter—the planning of new, flexible residential outgrowth? Habraken (1976), for example, considers the principle to be one of his most important concepts in developing a theory for mass housing. Though the application was made in an urban setting, the principles he developed are instructive, in that he defined the hierarchical division as one that differentiates between the role of the community and the role of the individual in creating housing. The absence of this role distinction, he claims, will result in the "perfect barracks" of mass housing as offered by high-rise urban projects. In an attempt to sidestep the possibility of such monotonous failure, he engaged the residents of his mass housing in the process of design and delivery (Habraken 1976; Dluhosch 1976).

Robert and Rebecca Oxman also applied the hierarchical principle on the urban scale in their design for a residential development in Haifa, Israel. They designed a self-sufficient, fully configured neighbourhood unit that was intended to be the building block of a city, much in the same way that Hershman and Mansfeld (as mentioned in Chapter 3) were doing at this time. The Oxmans' urban growth model is shown in Figure 5.2. The weakness of their planning, as with Hershman's and Mansfeld's, is the rigidity of implementation of the principle. In prescribing physical built form rather than hierarchical relationships of elements, it is assumed that such form, sufficient for present conditions, will also be sufficient in an unforeseeable future. Hierarchical categorization must be present as a guide to urban outgrowth by outlining the components of the development, their sequence of importance, and the ultimate relationships of components to each other and to the composition as a whole.

With these principles in mind, a description will be presented of the current planning procedures and their inherent weaknesses, followed by an alternative process to designing and processing flexible residential outgrowth.

Before the construction of a new suburban development on formerly vacant land can begin, the proposed design and all its components must pass through a lengthy approval process that usually requires acceptance at the municipal or provincial level,

or sometimes both. Development in rapidly growing suburban areas frequently takes place in 160- or 200-acre blocks (64 or 80 hectares) based on original farm surveys. These parcels are planned using some form of a secondary or district plan that establishes roads, parks, open spaces, and neighbourhood facilities in a general way, leaving the exact location of streets and blocks to subdivision control. The exact procedure through which these plans pass varies by province and state. The process of plan approval called subdivision control (or subdivision regulation) is a fundamental tool for land development. Although subdivision control is a powerful tool in its own right, it is not the only mechanism for development control. Land use, minimum lot size, and the bulk of structures to be built must conform to existing zoning legislation (Platt 1996). In many cases, the area to be developed is not of the desired zoning (for example, it may still be zoned agricultural), and therefore applicable amendments to the zoning act must first be obtained.

Besides satisfying zoning provisions, subdivision approval requires that the proposed development meet performance standards in terms of layout and design. The first step in developing formerly vacant land, therefore, requires submission of a detailed subdivision plan. A subdivision plan is very precise. It must "show exactly the proposed property lines, street system, water and sewer lines, and topographic changes to the site," as well as areas set aside for parks, schools, walkways, and shopping areas (Hodge 1998). The municipality examines this plan carefully, because as soon as

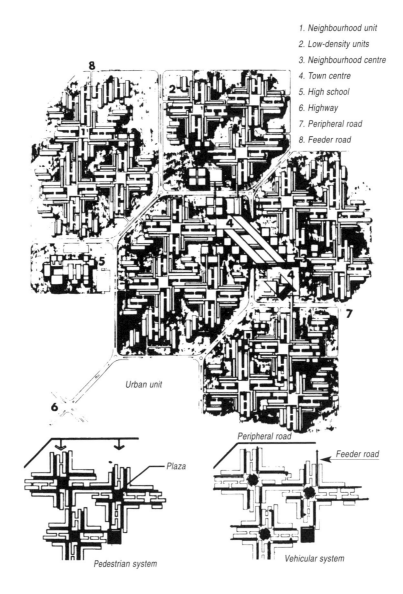

1. Neighbourhood unit
2. Low-density units
3. Neighbourhood centre
4. Town centre
5. High school
6. Highway
7. Peripheral road
8. Feeder road

Urban unit

Plaza

Pedestrian system

Peripheral road

Feeder road

Vehicular system

Figure 5.2. Much like Hershman's and Mansfeld's designs for Israeli developments, the Oxmans' is also the composition of a whole by identically designed neighbourhood units. Though hierarchically planned, the specificity with which built elements are articulated limits the proposal (Oxman and Oxman 1975).

it approves the plan, the municipality assumes responsibility for the subdivision.

As mentioned, specifics vary considerably by jurisdiction. However, the common features of subdivision control procedures in a Canadian context follow a general pattern. The *specified process* includes the application for approval, in which the form of the application, the steps of plan review, and the timeline are delineated. Under *plan circulation*, a draft version of the subdivision plan is circulated broadly for comment and recommendation. Applicable provincial departments, local government, and utility companies will review the plan. During the *conditions for approval* stage, the subdivider has an obligation to account for the roads, parks, and public utilities necessary for the subdivision. Since they will ultimately come under community ownership, their standards and how they will be paid for are specified here. The subdivision standards (or regulations) are central to subdivision control, as they examine the actual design of the proposed development with relation to the form and density of housing, street systems, open space, and essential community services. The *subdivision agreement* allows the municipality to ensure the staging of development, provision of services, road standards, minimum construction and material standards, and conveyance of land for parks. The *final subdivision plan*, after receiving approval, is registered and binds all future landowners (Hodge 1998).

Most provinces allow the community to establish conditions regarding the staging of the development so that it will coincide with its own plans and desires. Since some of the work promised by the subdivider may not be completed for years, the community can safeguard itself against potential losses in a variety of ways, for example, by requiring the developer to provide a bond to the city, or by imposing restrictive covenants on each lot (Platt 1996).

The next stage in new suburban development is the acquisition of a building permit. During this stage, the plan is evaluated on its compliance with fire and safety standards (as outlined in the national and supplementary building codes that apply to the area). Only after following this lengthy bureaucratic approval pathway can physical work begin on a suburban development.

Obviously, proceeding through these stages of review takes time—often a great deal of time. For instance, a housing design that won the Canadian Healthy House Competition was under review for over two years before eventually being approved (CMHC 1992). Though the house, now in Toronto, incorporated some of the most innovative energy conservation techniques of the time, a convoluted approval procedure kept it off the market initially. This unresponsiveness is one of the current planning procedure's most glaring weaknesses. By requiring such a great period of time between a project's inception and its execution, market demand is crippled. Although subdivision plans have some flexibility in relation to dwelling types (as long as they fall under the requirements outlined in the zoning plan), a developer is forced either to speculate as to what housing types will be needed in the next five to ten to fifteen years (or how-ever long the development construction is scheduled to take) or to design for present demands, which, as seen in an established neighbourhood in Chapter 4, are constantly and unpredictably shifting.

At the same time that the developer is prevented from making any kind of physical advances during this lag-time, the developer may also be losing money on mortgage payments and land taxes. Moreover, a developer whose financial or strategic situation changes over time would be burdened with a land investment whose use is predetermined and terribly inflexible.

Conventional planning wisdom may view the protracted nature of the approval process as an advantage. It slows down a project long enough so that anybody who might in some way be affected by it has a chance to voice his or her opinions. This is not a bad thing. However, as the review procedure stands today, it limits a development's ability to respond to market demands and can result in the production of inappropriate housing form.

A new design and approval procedure is required, in which sufficient review is still of the utmost importance but at the same time housing form can more closely follow changes in demands caused by societal evolution (whether due to demographic, economic, or technological issues). This can be achieved by simply breaking down a project's design in accordance with the anticipated construction schedule and the hierarchical component principles discussed above. By designing and proposing only one small section of a larger development (composed of numerous hierarchically organized constituent parts)—provided that financing and construction issues have been resolved—architects and planners would be able to design relevant housing for true social demand.

In fact, this hierarchical fragmentation of the development procedure, as outlined in Figure 5.3 and addressed in the remainder of this chapter, would benefit all parties involved. The developer and planner would create housing that is in high demand; the municipality would be able to control development according to its current ideals; and consumers would benefit from housing that is not only appropriate but cheaper than that of a development that for years has been losing money in taxes while in review.

Before looking at the proposed process, it is important to understand that along with the new design and approval procedure would naturally come changes in the way suburban developments are guided by municipal-level controls. These changes will also be addressed, step by step, as they relate to the new, more flexible development process.

Early in this new development process, developers, having acquired a large plot of land, would begin by formulating, together with planners, a vision of the kind of community that they expect to build. The vision would be based on, among other features, the character of the community in which the development is proposed, as well as on anticipated market

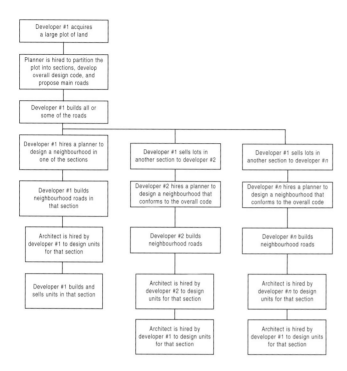

```
Developer #1 acquires
a large plot of land

Planner is hired to partition the
plot into sections, develop
overall design code, and
propose main roads

Developer #1 builds all or
some of the roads

Developer #1 hires a planner to        Developer #1 sells lots in           Developer #1 sells lots in
design a neighbourhood in              another section to developer #2      another section to developer #n
one of the sections

Developer #1 builds                    Developer #2 hires a planner to      Developer #n hires a planner to
neighbourhood roads in                 design a neighbourhood that          design a neighbourhood that
that section                           conforms to the overall code         conforms to the overall code

Architect is hired by                  Developer #2 builds                  Developer #n builds
developer #1 to design units           neighbourhood roads                  neighbourhood roads
for that section

Developer #1 builds and                Architect is hired by                Architect is hired by
sells units in that section            developer #2 to design               developer #n to design
                                       units for that section               units for that section

                                       Architect is hired by                Architect is hired by
                                       developer #1 to design units         developer #1 to design units
                                       for that section                     for that section
```

Figure 5.3. A process of designing and developing a suburban district such as this one allows for greater flexibility in terms of the final built form. Instead of there being only one design and one developer, market demands are met in as many ways as a project can be realized.

demand. This first step is similar to the definition of vision discussed in Chapter 4, as it relates to built form, open space, and circulation. The vision should be general, to allow for alternatives in built form and services, but adequately descriptive, so that it begins to define community character.

Returning to the concept of hierarchical characterization, next comes the task of articulating the key elements of the design. The major roads traversing the site, with their accompanying infrastructure, will to a great extent articulate the overall capacity of the development. The overall capacities and specifications of this major road element will be informed generally by the three aspects of the vision. It would be disadvantageous at this point, though, to dictate the form of all roads to be built on site over the duration of the project; prescribing the arterial roads and leaving the design of collectors and locals to a later date is sufficient. The hierarchical structure of the development cannot be so rigid that it precludes lateral flexibility within the layers of that hierarchical structure. In composing the major elements of the design, a concept of the final design is articulated.

At the next level of hierarchical importance is the determination of the shapes, sizes, and number of subsections into which the development will be divided. The massing of density of building would be determined within a general layout of the roads. The location of civic centres and greenbelts would also be specified. These determinations would all be part of the overall planning concept for the entire development. Currently, such determinations are sometimes outlined by the municipality in a secondary plan that deals with only a portion of the spatial area covered by the official, or master, plan (Ontario Ministry of Municipal Affairs 1989).

Though articulating a broad vision and roughly defining a neighbourhood concept are important initial steps, they would not by themselves ensure a harmonious community if development occurs in widely separate stages. To secure a certain degree of control in this respect, the planner at this stage would

Urban Level	Number of Units
District / Quarter	500 to 1,000
Neighbourhood	100 to 500
Cluster	60 to 80
Group of units	Up to 15
Dwelling unit	Single unit

Figure 5.4. Following the principle of hierarchical characterization, there would be five divisions of the overall suburban scale. As one moves up the scale, several of the lower components would make up the larger component one step directly above.

write a design code for the entire development. The code would be more descriptive than specific. For example, it would not demand a certain building height limitation, but it would discourage the building of high-rises unless provisions were made to prevent overloading infrastructure, creating abnormally high traffic flow, or casting shadows on neighbouring buildings. The code would also follow the initial vision of the development.

At this point, documentation of the community vision, the design of the primary hierarchical elements (concept), and the design code would be submitted to municipal authorities. This would be the first stage in a new approval procedure, whereby the character and other issues of the intended development could be reviewed by officials and residents of the municipality. It would also be possible at this point, though not necessary, to submit to the municipality fully designed and detailed proposals for subsections, conforming to the design code. In this way, broader development issues would be examined thoroughly and, once approved, would provide a framework for the evaluation of the subsections. Since the subsections are a great deal smaller than an entire master plan and are based on an approved vision and design code, they could then pass through the review process more rapidly.

Hierarchically, each subsection might actually be large enough so that it would be further divided into sub-subsections. An example of a development's hierarchical division, as defined by building number, is shown in Figure 5.4. In Figure 5.5, the

manner in which increments of growth occur along a suburban street is schematically illustrated.

It is important to stipulate that the original owner of the proposed site should be free to sell divided portions of the site to secondary developers, as is frequently the case at present. Though in the short term procedures will be more complex because of multiple owners of a single development, in the long term a more diverse and appropriate housing pattern will result with increased market competition. Having several developers in one site will ensure a community with a good mix of housing types and residences.

The hierarchical organization of different scales of suburban components, shown in Figure 5.5, not only determines the sequence of planning and decision making but also can begin to inform the process by which architectural controls can be

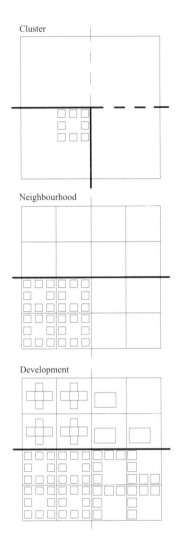

Figure 5.5. With the passage of time, a suburban street would develop incrementally so that a development is finally composed of neighbourhoods composed of clusters; all are laid out along primary and secondary street patterns.

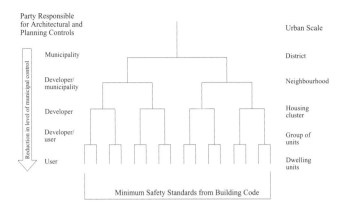

Figure 5.6. With the narrowing in scale, municipal control would lessen. At the dwelling unit level, responsibility for acting within architectural controls would fall to the owner of the unit. It is important to note, however, that minimum safety standards according to the appropriate building code must be upheld and are the responsibility of the municipality at all levels.

implemented along these different scales. This concept is illustrated schematically in Figures 5.6 and 5.7.

At the subsection or neighbourhood level, a second design code would be established. This is to safeguard against the erection by two independent developers of vastly contrasting buildings side by side, each conforming to the primary design code but interpreting it differently. The first developer to build in each subsection or neighbourhood of the development would be required to hire a planner and establish a secondary, more controlling design code. Guided by the general code, more specific dimensional and typological requirements would be established. As mentioned in Chapter 1, the work of Duany and Plater-Zyberk at Seaside, Florida, is a fine example of the manner in which a secondary design code would function. The code

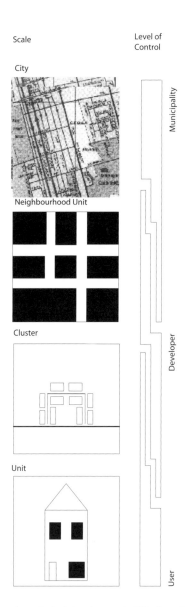

Scale

City

Neighbourhood Unit

Cluster

Unit

Level of
Control

Municipality

Developer

User

Figure 5.7. Though control of development shifts from the municipality, at a large scale, to a developer, at a medium scale, to the owner, at a very small scale, this is a gradual transition in the interests of keeping open communication between all parties involved.

	GENERAL DEVELOPMENT CODE	NEIGHBORHOOD CODE
SITE PLANNING AND URBAN DEVELOPMENT	• Range of building heights • Density • Building types	• Specific height limitations • Specific setbacks • Massing requirements • Architectural features
CIRCULATION/PARKING	• Major roads only • Sizing of roads and infrastructure	• Specific parking requirements • Access to parking • Parking location • Pedestrian paths
OUTDOOR LIVING SPACE	• General location • General characteristics • Proximity to different neighbourhoods	• Desired character • Proximity to residences • Proximity to roads • Desired ecology
IDENTITY AND IMAGE	• Demarcations between subdivisions • Recurring landmarks	• Neighbourhood streetscape • Palette vegetation • Building materials • Recurring building features

Figure 5.8. At the subsection level there would be two codes guiding development in order to ensure that conflicting built environments are not constructed. This is one of the main methods of control in the hands of the initial developer of the subsection.

allows for freedom of individual expression, according to needs at each discrete phase of construction, but should ensure that the nature of building form in subsections or neighbourhoods would not vary widely. An example of the contents of the primary and secondary codes is shown in Figure 5.8.

The proposed planning of new suburban growth, in which there would be a design code for an entire development accompanied by a more detailed secondary code for each subsection, does not imply a wholesale rejection of current planning codes. Architectural and planning control mechanisms ensure the safety of citizens as a result of a century's worth of study and experimentation. Though laws are added and removed, the sum of any current code, based on historical data, provides society with a very basic level of security. Even though they substantially reduce the range of design variety, they simply cannot be wiped off the books.

Because of the systematic nature of architectural codes, it would seem that the verification of a design's compliance with the applicable codes is a slow process. The same characteristic that makes the approval process slow, however, is one that could potentially liberate it from municipal red tape. To a great extent, the approval process is a check on whether or not various codes are respected. However, since the building codes and other control mechanisms are used as references throughout the process, checking them seems a somewhat redundant exercise.

In the interest of creating and reviewing a new, responsive suburbia, a new system of checks and balances is called for. At the heart of this new system is the assumption that planners and architects are trained professionals versed in the legislation and controls that apply to their specialty. To hold them responsible for adherence to such codes naturally follows. These two simple assumptions are not outrageous, but up to this point municipalities have not been willing to make them. If the municipality were to do this, acting in good faith prior to construction, a great time-consuming burden would be lifted from the shoulders of the reviewing body. Outlined in Figure 5.9 is the altered role that municipalities would play in the approval process. It is not suggested that the municipality step back and turn a blind eye to the execution of projects within its jurisdiction. To balance the lifting of this great responsibility

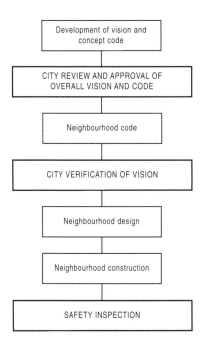

Figure 5.9. Architectural control will exist throughout the construction phase of the development. Surprise inspections are one method of maintaining compliance among developers with the standards set earlier by the municipality.

from the municipality, rigorous inspections would be conducted during and following the construction phase of the suburb. Should the development be found not to comply with the appropriate codes, a system of punitive fines would be levied, coupled with the responsibility to fix the non-conforming member. It is hoped that the possibility of such costly consequences would deter developers from building with uninformed or less-than-noble intentions.

In return for the added responsibility that planners and developers would carry, they would be awarded greater flexibility of final built form. And though developers would be governed by numerous codes, the hierarchy of codes outlined in Figure 5.10 would allow for free expression while maintaining safety and harmony.

Through the linear hierarchical relationship of codes and development stages, continuity and harmony can be maintained in new suburban developments. Designed and regulated in stages, reflecting the pace of construction and the needs of society at the time, the new flexible suburb is one that allows residents to experience domestic life in highly relevant housing. The creation of such outgrowth is also less of a risk for planners and developers, and municipalities will benefit from full, healthy neighbourhoods for years to come.

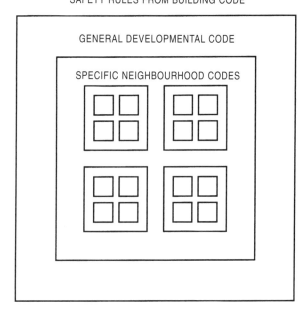

Figure 5.10. As the development is constructed on a smaller scale, more extensive and specific architectural controls to which building must conform are required by the proposed development and approval process.

The Experiment: La Prairie Development

A simulation will now be presented in which both the new design process and its theoretical basis have been implemented. The result should illustrate, in comparison with the current development method, the flexibility of the new process and a new adaptability in built form. The intention of the simulation is not to exclude or limit representation and interpretation of the proposed principles but rather to serve as a written and graphic guide in conveying one possible procedure and end product. The procedure will follow the steps outlined in the previous section of this chapter—beginning with the generation of the primary vision and ending with the actual design of two subsections, one by the primary developer and one by a secondary developer who has purchased a subsection from the primary developer. But first a brief profile of the existing community of La Prairie as well as the control mechanisms that currently apply to the experimental site are required. It is important to understand that though the development is proposed within the confines of the Municipality of La Prairie, a rigorous analysis of the site's existing surrounding character and demographics is not as vital to the definition of this project. Unlike the intervention described in Chapter 4, this site is one that at present has no built context.

La Prairie is a predominantly French-speaking municipality of 13,000 residents located along the south shore of the St. Lawrence River, approximately 10 km (6.3 miles) from downtown Montreal. Its location in relation to the island of Montreal

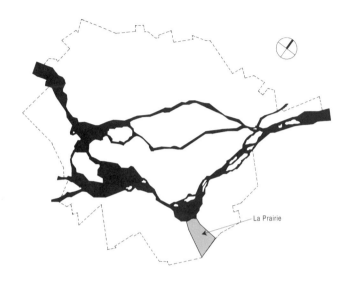

Figure 5.11. The municipality of La Prairie is located on the southern shore of the St. Lawrence River in Quebec. To a great extent, the character of the municipality is dictated by its relationship to the city of Montreal, on the main island.

is shown in Figure 5.11. It is bounded by the towns of Brossard and Candiac to the east and west, respectively; St. Philippe to the south, and the river to the north. A map of La Prairie at a smaller scale is shown in Figure 5.12.

Founded in 1647 as the farming Seignoiry of La Prairie de la Magdeleine, the community has grown from a dense mixed-use urban core along the river's edge to a series of predominantly residential developments inland. These developments can be divided into five identifiable residential housing

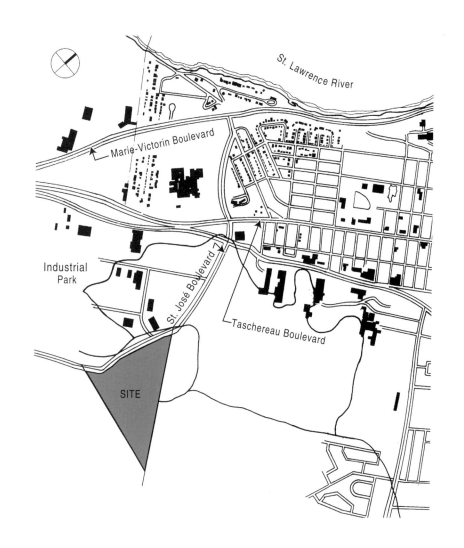

Figure 5.12. The site of the experiment is an irregularly shaped plot of undeveloped land set back from the river. The site and its adjacent districts are shown.

types. Along the river front, in the historic sector shown in Figure 5.13, there are a mixture of duplexes, triplexes, and single-family homes dating back to the eighteenth century.

The average price of these older homes is $100,000. To the east of the historic district are two newer residential sectors: La Citière and La Clarière. Both developments consist mainly of two-storey bungalows and cottages. La Citière, the older of the two, was built in 1977 and has an average housing price between $85,000 and $179,000. Construction of La Clarière began in 1984 and homes sell for between $150,000 and $200,000. Figure 5.14 shows some of this newer housing stock. The two remaining housing sectors, Le Grand Boise and La Magdeleine, are located further from the historic sector. Situated along the southeast edge of town, La Magdeleine consists of cottages and condominiums built throughout the 1980s. Le Grand Boise, located along the southwest edge of town, offers some of the most recently built housing. Construction of this sector—it contains mostly single-family homes—began in 1989.

The varied housing types found in La Prairie are good indicators of the demographic groups occupying them. Approximately 50% of the municipality's population consists of middle- to upper-income groups, occupying newer single-family detached homes. This group includes two-parent, white-collar families with one or two children and middle-aged households. A second group, the salaried blue-collar workers, account for 29% of the population and occupy mainly

Figure 5.13. Older housing and historically significant buildings can be found on the shore of the St. Lawrence in La Prairie. The site of the simulated project is far enough removed from this area that land prices are not affected by proximity.

Figure 5.14. Housing from the La Clarière and La Citière developments are shown here. Such housing is significantly more expensive than the housing proposed for the simulation.

townhouses, apartments, and multiplex housing. Approximately 15% of the population consists of working-class groups, including unmarried men or low-income couples with one or two children, and the elderly. This segment of the population owns or rents the multiple-housing units in the community.

The principal industries of La Prairie are light and heavy manufacturing as well as retail and commerce.

The site chosen for the simulation is an irregular, triangle-shaped 11.6-hectare (29-acre) piece of vacant land located along the southwest edge of the municipality of La Prairie. The land is bounded by an industrial park on the northwest and by a series of power lines to the southeast. The site's proximity to both a major traffic artery and a bus line, its location with respect to downtown Montreal, and its low land value make it an appealing location for development. Figure 5.15 shows the site's current state and some of its adjacent areas.

In 1991, the municipality of La Prairie adopted its master plan. By the following February, its policies were being fully implemented. The goal of the document was to establish a series of guidelines that would act as a framework within which future town development could be regulated.

The master plan is accompanied by two more specific planning legislative documents: the Specific Urban Plan, which addresses how the future growth of downtown La Prairie should occur, and the Planned Unit Development (PUD), which deals with the development of larger tracts of residential land. (A PUD can be established when a developer proposes innovative

Figure 5.15. The site is totally undeveloped (bottom). Adjacent to the site are attached single-family dwellings (top).

standards that are not met under existing zoning regulations or applicable standards; for each project, a set of requirements are specifically established, sometimes relaxing certain standards, such as those relating to height and lot size.) Combined, these planning guidelines set specific criteria that guide the approval process for development in the town's jurisdiction. Rules are enforced by the planning department and municipal council, based upon the recommendations made by the Planning Consulting Committee, a council composed of five local citizens.

In the master plan are several sections relevant to the simulation. In the section that specifies land usage and density of different zones, a number of criteria intended to create integrated planning, stimulate economic development, and protect the environment are articulated. This section also includes policies that regulate the presence of daycare centres and housing for the elderly. It ensures compatibility between the industrial sector and the adjacent residential or commercial sectors. Because the municipality is composed of both agricultural and urban land, which is subdivided into an array of different land uses (the site in question, for instance, is a small part of the low-density residential sectors, which comprise only 40% of urban land use), ensuring that there is no conflict between adjacent sectors is no simple task.

All development, ranging from a request for a single building permit to the development proposal for a large tract of land, is subject to the approval process set up by the municipality. The process (outlined in Figure 5.16) begins with the presentation of a proposal to the municipality's Urban Planning Department. It should include land usage, density, and road system specifications. The plan is either rejected (and corrections must be made) or accepted. Once the proposal is approved, the developer may not alter it without going through the approval procedure again.

The planning mechanism Site Planning and Architectural Integration Programmes (SPAIP), enacted in 1993, further influences the approval procedure and ultimately the final form of the developed site. The SPAIP acts within the approval process to control the architectural quality of a project. In an area where projects are subject to the evaluation of the SPAIP, the developer is asked to submit specific planning and architectural drawings of each project to the city planning department. The proposal then goes through a similar approval procedure to the one mentioned in the simulation below, using predetermined evaluation criteria. Once the proposal is accepted, the developer is responsible for the execution of the project as specified. The main advantage of this is that the municipality has great control over the architectural character of new building.

Two existing conditions may influence the final form of the proposed development site. The first is an industrial park to the west of the site. Its immediate proximity to the study area requires that buffer zones be formed between industrial and residential sectors in order to maintain a harmonious

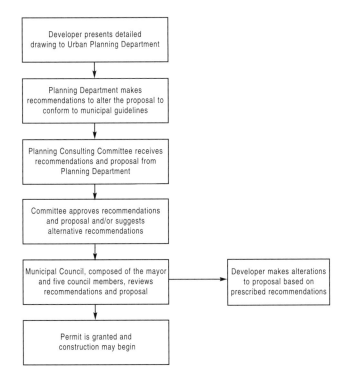

```
┌─────────────────────────────────┐
│  Developer presents detailed    │
│  drawing to Urban Planning      │
│  Department                     │
└─────────────────────────────────┘
              │
              ▼
┌─────────────────────────────────┐
│  Planning Department makes      │
│  recommendations to alter the   │
│  proposal to conform to         │
│  municipal guidelines           │
└─────────────────────────────────┘
              │
              ▼
┌─────────────────────────────────┐
│  Planning Consulting Committee  │
│  receives recommendations and   │
│  proposal from Planning         │
│  Department                     │
└─────────────────────────────────┘
              │
              ▼
┌─────────────────────────────────┐
│  Committee approves             │
│  recommendations and proposal   │
│  and/or suggests alternative    │
│  recommendations                │
└─────────────────────────────────┘
              │
              ▼
┌─────────────────────────────┐      ┌──────────────────────┐
│ Municipal Council, composed │─────▶│ Developer makes      │
│ of the mayor and five       │      │ alterations to       │
│ council members, reviews    │      │ proposal based on    │
│ recommendations and proposal│      │ prescribed           │
│                             │      │ recommendations      │
└─────────────────────────────┘      └──────────────────────┘
              │
              ▼
┌─────────────────────────────────┐
│  Permit is granted and          │
│  construction may begin         │
└─────────────────────────────────┘
```

Figure 5.16. The approval process, as outlined by the Ville de la Prairie Zoning Regulations (1992), begins with the submission of a master plan to the municipality's Urban Planning Department. After several review stages, either the plan is accepted and a permit for construction is granted or the plan is rejected and the process must start again at the drawing board.

relationship between adjacent uses. The second is the particularities of site zoning. The experimental site has been zoned as a residential and community sector, stipulating that single-family houses that are detached, semi-detached, or attached be the range of housing types. A maximum gross density of 30 dwellings per hectare (12 per acre) has been recommended. Figure 5.17 outlines the principal zoning bylaws that apply to the experimental site. Alternatively, the site may be developed as an integrated plan. This means that should a developer find the existing guidelines to be too restrictive for the type of development he intends to propose, an alternative master plan may be presented for the site that augments existing guidelines or proposes new ones.

The principal concept behind the design proposal of the simulation was the creation of a series of diverse housing types set around a large linear community green space. This green space follows the contour of the creek that runs through a portion of the site. In an attempt to link both the adjacent and peripheral housing to the public green, a series of pedestrian paths were introduced. Many of these paths are continuations of pedestrian paths in the areas surrounding the site, and are intended to integrate the new development with those around it. A site analysis of the existing conditions was made and is shown in Figure 5.18.

In addition to exploring the new planning procedure, a primary concern was the creation of affordable housing in a low-rise, medium-density suburban area. This meant designing

Figure 5.17. Some of the principal zoning bylaws pertaining to the study site are shown here (Ville de la Prairie 1992).

Building and lot sizes

▸ Building types consist of detached and semi-detached residential units.

▸ Both the minimum and maximum heights of dwellings are two storeys.

▸ Parking is limited to one to two spaces per single-family unit.

▸ Multi-family units are allocated 1.5 parking spaces per dwelling.

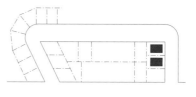

Lot orientation

▸ Lateral lot lines must be perpendicular to the road. Deviation from this is allowed in the case where lot lines may be oblique to achieve the required lot size.

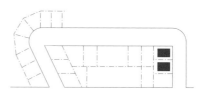

Width of residential block

▸ Residential blocks must be wide enough to accommodate two rows of lots back to back.

▸ Minimum width of street block is 60 m.

Length of street block

▸ For street blocks not bisected by a pedestrian path (L1), minimum length is 75 m and maximum length is 360 m.

▸ For street blocks bisected by a pedestrian path (L2), minimum length is 75 m and maximum length is 550 m.

▸ Minimum width of pedestrian path is 3 m.

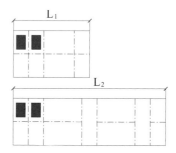

Figure 5.18. An initial site analysis is important in designing new suburban fabric that is well integrated with the rest of the municipality. Such factors as views, prevailing wind directions, and geographic characteristics have been considered in the analysis of the La Prairie site.

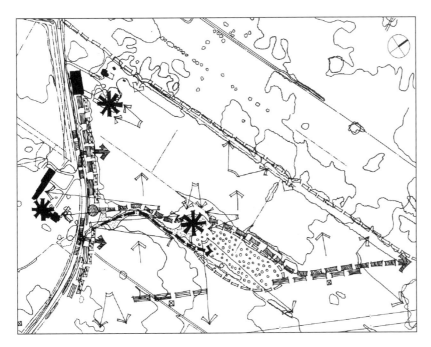

Proposed view sheds (to other communities and visual attractions such as farmhouse and vegetation)

Proposed view screening

Proposed focal points

Proposed retention of vegetation communities

Best location for stormwater retention area

Proposed retention of creek

Proposed vehicular circulation connection to future road

Proposed pedestrian link to wooded land/recreation path

Proposed pedestrian link to transit system

Windscreen needed

Building alignment to minimize exposure to electromagnetic fields (maximize buffer zone between Hydro right of way and buildings) small, compact dwellings (100 to 150 m^2 [1,000 to 1,500 ft^2]), reducing lot sizes by using semi-detached and rowhouse arrangements, and developing efficient street layouts that would reduce infrastructure costs while making effective use of open space. The heritage of old La Prairie was considered in the design of new units. There was also an intention to design units that easily permit alterations and additions, similar to the Cape Cod houses seen in Chapter 4. The final program was developed for approximately 300 dwelling units with a price range of $75,000 to $85,000.

The hierarchical organization of the project begins with the main traffic route that loops around the interior of the site and from which radiate smaller secondary roads. Both of these primary and secondary roads are lined with a variety of two-storey townhouses, semi-detached houses, and detached houses. Figures 5.19 and 5.20 show the conceptual organization of the plan and its major components at this point in the planning procedure.

The low cost of land at the study site (a result of marginal location, odd shape, and proximity to an industrial area) allowed for the creation of affordable housing, though it presented a marketing problem. Therefore, using the land prices of 1993 ($7 per square foot) and development charges ($400 per foot of frontage), a "community" rather than a "development" was designed. This meant paying special attention to the supplementary factors that contribute to the convenience and comfort of residents. The intended result of the new planning procedure, which will be addressed in the rest of this chapter, is a cohesive and integrated community.

The goal of the development is to create a diverse physical environment. The community will consist of a series of distinct spaces that unfold as the user moves through them. The spaces will consist of neighbourhood-like areas and landscaped open spaces containing a variety of vegetation and street furniture. A range of low-rise housing types (no more than six storeys) will be offered, varying in character and price. The community should encourage a mix of commercial enterprises, such as a recreation centre, café, daycare, and business supply store. The various subdivisions of the community should be united by a commonly shared built element or open space, such as gathering halls or public greens. This will help foster and reinforce a certain degree of cohesion and the overall sense of community. Streets should be laid out to encourage walking and pleasant views. Short blocks, sidewalks, and tree-lined roads will help create a human scale in the development. Finally, residential units should have direct access to either semi-public or private outdoor living space. Figure 5.21 shows some sketches that could be used in conjunction with the development and presentation of the community at a broad level.

The planner then generates a number of alternative design strategies and codes that reflect the vision that was adopted earlier for the site and that conform to the appropriate municipal master plan. The developer selects the design

Figure 5.19. At this point, major hierarchical elements are documented at a very conceptual level. The configuration of the major roads as well as the possible housing types and densities are shown in this organizational plan (after Alnemer et al. 1993).

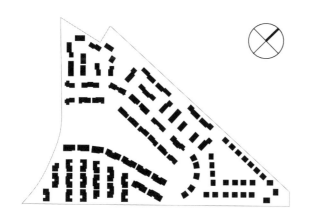

Built areas

Housing Types	Number of units (294)	Dimensions of units (metres)	Lot size (metres)
Townhouse with private parking	180	6 x 12	6 x 24
Condominium with common parking	30	6 x 12	6 x 24
Semi-detached with private parking	48	4.5 x 9 4.5 x 12	7.5 x 24 7.5 x 24

Area (hectares)	Density (units/hectare)	Linear dimension of road (metres)	Number of parking lots
11.6	25.4 (gross)	645 (collector)	274 (88%) (private)
	35.5 (net)	1,160 (local)	38 (12%) (common)

Project information

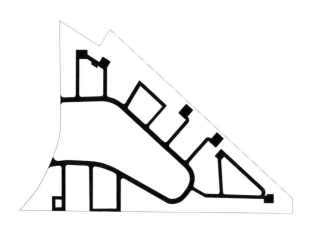

Streets

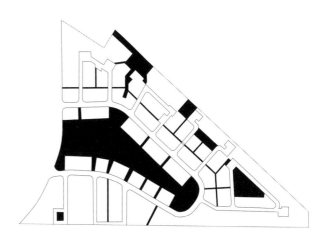

Public open space

Figure 5.20. Also contained in the conceptual plan are the major subdivisions of the development and short written descriptions of how the built form was generated and how the proposed community will interact with built form and site characteristics. Note that the experimental site has been divided into four subsections, **A** through **D**.

Public Green Space

The generating idea is to create a public green space around which the community will develop. The choice to centre the community around a public green is an attempt to tie the developer's vision of using a public space to unite the various phases of development and thus help to foster a sense of community. Since there are limited views outward from the site, the open space serves to orient the community inwards as well as create pleasant views for users. Finally, a series of pedestrian paths will lead users into and through the open space.

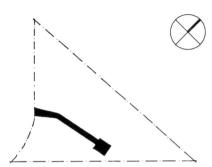

Main Collector Street

This particular collector road pattern was chosen for a number of reasons. Its overall form offers a sensitive gesture to the natural environment by contouring around the existing creek and green space. The uniform arrangement facilitates the subdivision of the site as well as the layout of such infrastructure components as sewage, water, and electrical grids. The limited curvilinear form of the road further ensures easy visual and physical access into and through the site by both vehicle and pedestrian traffic. The subdivision of the site into smaller blocks is an attempt to create a human scale and a diverse environment.

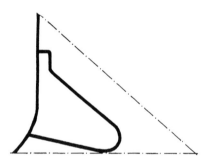

Subdivision of Development

The size of the subdivisions within the larger site was based on the developer's desire to limit the number of dwelling and commercial units that could occupy a given area. The developer felt that current market demand for the low-rise residential dwelling he proposes dictates a subdivision that could sustain approximately 80 to 100 units, a parcel of land sufficient for a first run of houses. The sequential arrangement of subdivisions was chosen for its ability to facilitate development expansion for smaller runs of dwellings while minimizing infrastructure costs.

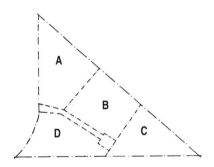

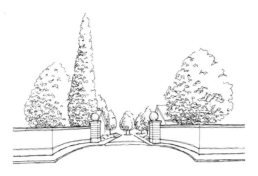

*Design a series of distinct views that unfold as a
person moves through a neighborhood unit*

*Use architectural and natural elements to create
streets that encourage walking*

Plant trees at vista points

Reduce front setbacks and road width

Place special buildings at intersections

*Create housing units that have direct access
to private outdoor living space*

Figure 5.21. Some aspects of the proposed community vision can be presented using sketches. In addition to furthering the development design, such drawings are an unambiguous way to present the character of the community to a municipal review committee.

that corresponds with the vision of the site and presents it to the city planning department for approval. The city renders a decision only after verifying that the code and plans meet the minimum standards for public safety, regarding site accessibility by fire, medical, and police vehicles; quality of life, assuring that there are no conflicting adjacent land uses and that there is sufficient public access to light and air; and infrastructure specifications.

A new code is then developed based on the vision and concept that have been approved by the municipal authorities. An example of one possible code for the simulation is shown in Figure 5.22.

The developer continues by selecting one or several subsections to be developed in the very near future. A detailed design concept and building code are then developed for the selected parcels of land, making sure that they conform to a previously determined set of development codes. Once the developer accepts the neighbourhood unit design and codes by which the developer will build, a graphically documented proposal, similar to Figure 5.23, is presented to the municipal planning department for verification. After it has been verified that all concept and safety codes have been addressed, the municipality grants the developer a building permit. If requirements have not been met, the municipality rejects the plan until appropriate changes have been made.

Figures 5.24 and 5.25 illustrate the developer-initiated deed restrictions that would enforce all neighbourhood unit codes.

If the initial developer decides to partition and sell off some of the remaining subsections of the site, the second developer on the site is responsible, through previously established planning, for maintaining a certain degree of continuity with the existing development. This second developer is then required to create a neighbourhood unit development design and code for his subdivision. The graphically documented proposal is presented to the municipal planning department for verification. The municipality, having in its possession the vision, concept, and schematic master plan, verifies that this secondary proposal is acceptable and verifies that the public safety standards and minimum infrastructure specifications are met. The municipality then grants the developer a building permit or asks that necessary changes to the proposal be made. This entire process could be carried out in a fraction of the time that traditional planning procedures would require. Figures 5.26, 5.27, and 5.28 show the documentation that the second developer on the experimental site would be responsible for presenting before a construction permit is granted.

The incremental process of design and submission would continue until all subsections have been fully developed. In this manner, a diverse and healthy community, full of highly appropriate housing, can be created. It would be a community that is well integrated with the municipality in which it is located, and whose constituent parts relate harmoniously to each other. In all respects, a community such as this, generated from a new design and approval procedure, would benefit municipalities, developers, and residents of North American suburbia.

Figure 5.22. At this stage, a code based on the vision and concept is written by the planner of the community. It begins to specify aspects of the design that are only indicated by the preceding diagrammatic plan (Fig. 5.21). Such aspects would range from the parking allotments to the building footprints to the demarcation of public open spaces.

Site Planning and Built Environment

▸ Total FAR (floor area ratio): 0.8-1.5.

▸ Maximum gross density: 50-70 units/hectare.

▸ Total number of units: 550-650 units.

▸ Infrastructure (sewage, water, and electricity systems) are to be designed to capacity for FAR.

▸ No built structure shall exceed six storeys.

▸ Buildings shall be a minimum and a maximum of 7 m from right of way.

▸ There shall be no height restrictions on structures whose footprint is less than 40 m^2.

Circulation and Parking

Roads

▸ Collector roads are to be 9 m wide as well as maintain 1 m planting surfaces on both sides.

▸ Secondary roads shall maintain a minimum width of 4 m and a maximum of 7 m.

▸ All road surfaces shall be paved.

▸ All roads shall be lined with trees at intervals of no less than 10 m.

Parking

▸ Parking on all collector streets is allowed.

▸ Minimum parking on private lots: 1 parking spot/unit.

▸ All on-surface parking lots shall contain no more than 2 vehicular parking spots.

▸ All private parking spots may be either indoors or outdoors.

Pedestrian Circulation

▸ Paths shall be a minimum width of 3 m and a maximum width of 5 m.

▸ The maximum distance from each house to public transportation shall not be more than 1,500 m.

Outdoor Living Areas and Outdoor Spaces

▸ All subdivisions shall allot between 10% and 15% of total land area for outdoor public and/or semi-private spaces.

▸ Each outdoor space shall contain a children's playground with a minimum area of 3% of the total outdoor area.

Community Identity and Image

▸ A clear demarcation between neighbourhood unit developments shall be encouraged.

▸ This may be achieved by but not be limited to:
  • the use of gates and fences to separate subdivisions
  • the planting of trees around subdivision boundaries
  • the type and arrangement of street furniture and amenities

▸ To create focal points, all public and semi-private open spaces shall be identified with physical markers.

Figure 5.23. Based on the previously submitted planning documents for the entire development, a design plan, such as the one shown here for plot A of the experimental site, is submitted for one subsection of the larger development.

Roads

The generating idea for the neighbourhood unit development is to create a semi-public green space that is bordered by and unites the various housing units in the subdivision. The secondary road system employed wraps around and defines the green space or "square" in an attempt to create an intimate and distinct community setting. The short cul-de-sac configuration of the road contributes to the developer's global vision of creating roads that make vistas and encourage walking. The juxtaposition of secondary roads to each other as well as to the collector road results in shorter, more human-scale blocks. The limited area for which each road is responsible reduces the cost of laying out such infrastructure components as sewage, water, and electrical systems.

Built Form

The housing structures and patterns chosen respond to the developer's intention to build between 80 and 100 affordable low-rise housing units that cater to first-time home buyers. The construction of attached town-houses and condominium units will make the dwelling affordable while maintaining a sense of individual ownership through such features as private parking, entrances, and outdoor living areas. The layout of buildings along both the main collector and secondary roads as well as around the open space creates a strong street edge that encourages walking. The orientation of such building openings as windows and doors towards the street and open space increases safety by ensuring unobstructed visual and physical access to these spaces.

Open Space

The open space provides a distinct area that defines the neighbourhood by uniting the various housing units around it and focusing public activity within it. While the semi-public space may be used by adjacent neighbourhood unit developments, the intent is to provide a public forum for the users in the immediate vicinity. The use of both soft and hard surfaces to compose the semi-public open space encourages a variety of activities such as children's playgrounds, reading niches, and picnic areas. Trees are planted on portions of the site to offer shade and around the perimeter of the neighbourhood to define and screen the area from adjacent neighbourhoods and land uses.

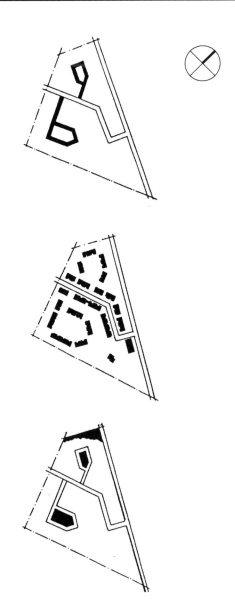

Figure 5.24. A document-type deed restriction for the community would control such architectural issues as dwelling height and type. The responsibility for implementation of such a control and its enforcement would fall mostly on the shoulders of the developer of the subsection.

Site Planning and Built Environment

There are three types of low-density residential dwellings:

Detached single-family units

▸ All exterior wall cladding shall be 60% brick and 40% wood.

Semi-detached units

▸ All exterior wall cladding shall be 60% brick and 40% wood.

Rowhouses

▸ All exterior wall cladding shall be 100% brick.

The following standards pertain to all dwelling types:

▸ Windows and doors shall be made of wood or vinyl-clad wood.

▸ The total glazing area on a facade shall not exceed 30% of the facade surface.

▸ Principal building roofs shall be symmetrically gabled or hipped, pitched between 4:12 and 8:12.

▸ Brick mortar joints shall be struck and no more than 50 mm wide.

Building height:

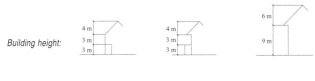

Building type:

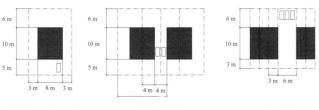

Detached single-family   *Semi-detached*   *Rowhouse*

Porches

▸ There should be a mandatory glazed or unglazed and roofed structure fronting the street.

▸ The minimum length of a front porch shall be a percentage of the building's street facade.

▸ Porches may be constructed of 40% wood and 60% brick.

Porch length:

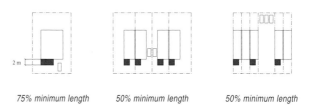

75% minimum length   *50% minimum length*   *50% minimum length*

Outbuildings

▸ An ancillary structure located within a designated yard area to serve such functions as home offices, apartments, or workshops.

▸ Outbuildings are permitted in the rear yards of all unit types.

▸ Outbuildings shall not exceed in height the principal structure.

▸ The walls of outbuildings placed on property lines shall be left windowless.

▸ All construction must conform to the National Building Code for Safety regarding the appropriate function it will serve.

▸ The pitch of an outbuilding roof shall not be less than 2:12.

Figure 5.24 continued

Circulation and Parking

Roads

▸ All secondary roads shall be paved in asphalt.

▸ Both primary and secondary roads shall be lined with maple trees.

▸ Secondary roads shall be 7 m wide.

Parking

▸ A mandatory clear area no less than 4 m by 6 m with a minimum 3 m wide continuous access to the street.

▸ Garages shall follow the specifications of outbuildings unless originally built into the design of the dwelling unit.

▸ A minimum of one private outdoor parking spot per unit.

▸ On-street parking directly fronting a lot shall count towards fulfilling the parking requirement (off-street parking is located as shown below):

Parking location:

Pedestrian Circulation

▸ All pedestrian crossing surfaces shall be made of cobblestone.

▸ For every 20 units of rowhouses, a pedestrian path 3 m wide shall be provided that passes through the block.

▸ All paths shall be lined with shrubs.

▸ All paths shall be lit with stainless steel street lamps that are spaced at a distance of 7 m.

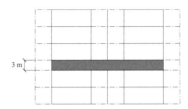

Outdoor Living Areas and Open Spaces

▸ Every 700 m² of public open space shall be provided with a garbage can.

▸ All paths through or into these spaces shall be lit by stainless steel street lamps spaced at a distance of 17 m.

▸ Each semi-private and public open space shall be covered with a minimum 35% of grass.

▸ All semi-public and public parks must be furnished with wooden benches (one bench per 15 m² of open space).

▸ All trees in public tracts shall be nursery-grown, ball and burlapped.

▸ All trees shall have a minimum of 200 mm caliper with a 5 m height.

Community Identity and Image

▸ A hedgerow of shrubs shall be planted along all subdivision lines.

▸ All shrubs shall be planted in groups of ten (of like species) rather than as individuals. (Minimum spacing: l m on centre for hedges, up to 2 m on centre maximum for open planting.)

▸ Planting in immediate proximity to buildings shall respect architectural lines.

▸ Planting towards the street should respect the integrity of the street.

Figure 5.24 continued

- Planting should not obscure the buildings and should respect views to and from the street, porches, walks, and public parks.
- Fences shall be made of wood pickets, lattice, or boards.
- Fences shall be made with no more than 100 mm gaps between pickets.
- Entrances to collector and secondary roads shall be marked by a stone wall as shown below:

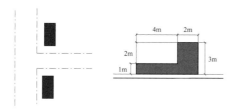

Entry gate feature: *Plan*   *Elevation*

Figure 5.25. The plans of the various neighbourhood units would also be documented in the deed restrictions of the subsection.

Front elevation

Unit plan options: upper level

Townhouse unit

Unit plan options: lower level

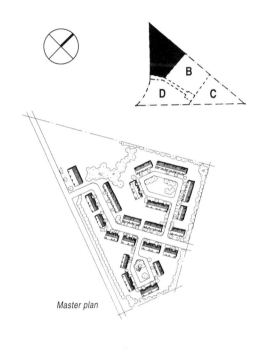

Master plan

Housing Types	Number of units (75)	Dimensions of units (metres)	Lot size (metres)
Townhouse with private parking	50	6 x 12	6 x 24
Condominium with common parking	25	6 x 12	6 x 24

Area (hectares)	Density (units/hectare)	Linear dimension of road (metres)	Number of parking lots
2	27 (gross)	160 (collector)	84 (100%) (private)
	37.5 (net)	310 (local)	

Project information

Roads

The architect of Developer Y chose to create an environment of individual low-rise single-family homes that share a public green space. The secondary road system employed circles the subdivision to maximize access to buildable land while defining and enclosing both the open space and built forms. The circuit pattern of the road facilitates pedestrian and vehicular movement through the neighbourhood while offering the users a continuously changing setting. Trees line the road, creating a buffer between pedestrian and automobile while reflecting the mandatory requirements for planting found in the development code. Finally, the road pattern chosen maximizes efficiency for the layout of infrastructure components.

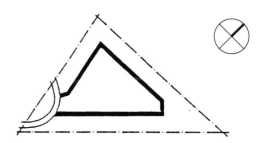

Built Form

The residential housing types designed for the development reflect the developer's interest in creating a small community of between 30 and 40 affordable low-rise single-family units. A sense of individual ownership is achieved through the use of detached dwellings with individual entrances, private backyards, and parking. The building's limited setback from the street, combined with its close proximity to adjacent homes and the choice to allocate off-surface parking to the side of each dwelling, helps create a strong street edge. Smaller outbuildings attached to the rear of each home offer multi-purpose spaces to their users.

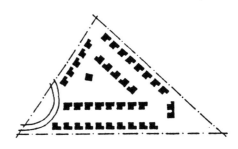

Open Space

Located along the edge of the neighbourhood unit, the semi-public outdoor space offers a public forum for the residents. Both hard and soft surfaces are used to create a place where people can gather to conduct a number of leisure activities, including a playground for children and eating and reading areas. Conforming to the development code pertaining to outdoor living areas, trees are planted in the green space and along the subdivision lot line. The trees flanking the edge of the neighbourhood insulate it from adjacent land uses while creating a clear demarcation between neighbourhood unit developments. A gazebo is placed in the open space, offering a focal point and an identifiable landmark for the residents.

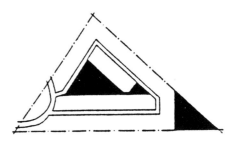

Figure 5.27. Deed restrictions developed by the second developer on the experimental site are used in conjunction with the plan, as seen in the previous subsection (Fig. 5.25). Though the quality of spatial and environmental content of the first and second developer's restrictions need not be identical, a certain continuity and compatibility are guaranteed because of their compliance with the original site documentation.

Site Planning and Built Environment

Residential housing type:

Detached Single-Family Home

The following standards pertain to all dwellings:

▶ Windows and doors shall be made of aluminum or vinyl-clad wood.

▶ The total glazing area on a facade shall not exceed 40% of the facade surface.

▶ Principal building roofs shall be symmetrically gabled between 4:12 and 8:12.

▶ All exterior cladding shall be 80% wood or vinyl and 20% brick.

▶ Bricks shall be arranged in a common running bond pattern.

▶ All construction must conform to the National Building Code for safety regarding the appropriate function it will serve.

▶ The pitch of an outbuilding roof shall not be less than 2:12.

▶ All exterior walls shall be clad in 100% wood only.

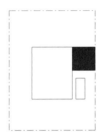

Minimum area: 45 m^2

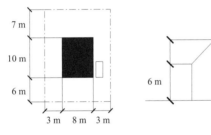

Building type:	Detached single-family	Building height

Outbuildings

▶ A mandatory ancillary structure located along and attached to either side of the principal dwelling.

▶ Outbuildings shall not exceed in height the principal structure.

▶ The walls of outbuildings placed on property lines shall be left windowless.

Circulation and Parking

Roads

▶ All secondary roads shall be paved in asphalt.

▶ Both primary and secondary roads shall be lined with maple trees.

▶ Secondary roads shall be 7 m wide.

Parking

▶ A mandatory clear area no less than 4 m by 6 m with a minimum 3 m wide continuous access to the street.

Figure 5.27 continued

- Garages shall follow the specifications of outbuildings.
- A minimum of two private outdoor parking spots per unit.
- On-street parking directly fronting a lot shall count towards fulfilling the parking requirement (off-street parking is located as shown below).

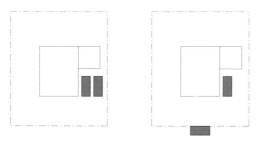

Parking location

Pedestrian Circulation

- All pedestrian crossing surfaces shall be made of cobblestone.
- All paths shall be a minimum and maximum width of 2 m.
- All paths shall be lined with shrubs.
- All paths shall be lit with steel street lamps that are spaced at a distance of 16 m.

Outdoor Living Areas and Open Spaces

- Every 700 m² of public open space shall be provided with a garbage can.
- All paths through or into these spaces shall be lit by steel street lamps spaced at a distance of 16 m.
- Each semi-private and public open space shall be covered with a minimum 50% of grass.

- All semi-public and public parks must be furnished with wooden benches (one bench per 15 m² of open space).
- All trees in public tracts shall be nursery-grown, ball and burlapped.
- All trees shall have a minimum of 200 mm caliper with a 5 m height.
- All private backyards shall be lined with picket fences.

Community Identity and Image

- A hedgerow of shrubs shall be planted along all subdivision lines.
- All shrubs shall be planted in groups of ten (of like species) rather than as individuals. (Minimum spacing: 1 m on centre for hedges, up to 2 m on centre maximum for open planting.)
- Planting in immediate proximity to buildings shall respect architectural lines.
- Planting towards the street should respect the integrity of the street.
- Planting should not obscure the buildings and should respect views to and from the street, porches, walks, and public parks.
- Fences shall be made of wood pickets, lattice, or boards.
- Fences shall be made with no more than 100 mm gaps between pickets.

Figure 5.28. The master plan and unit plans of subsection C should be included in the second developer's documentation.

Upper level plan

Ground floor plan

Front elevation

Housing unit   *Side elevation*

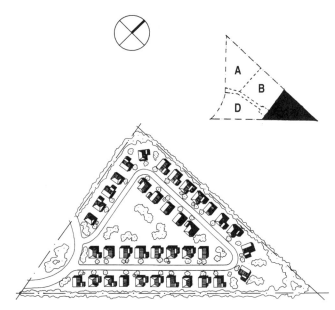

Master plan

Housing Types	Number of units (38)	Dimensions of units (metres)	Lot size (metres)
Detached single family with private parking	38	9 x 10	14 x 24

Area (hectares)	Density (units/hectare)	Linear dimension of road (metres)	Number of parking lots
3	7 (gross)	90 (collector)	100% (private)
	12.7 (net)	380 (local)	

Project information

The creation of a more responsive suburban fabric has been considered as it relates to the adaptation of older residential communities (Chapter 4) and the design of clean-slate developments (Chapter 5). In this chapter, we shall investigate the design of a segment of suburban fabric that can be gracefully integrated into an existing community in such a way that it provides a satisfying living environment for its residents and increases the overall livability of the established community.

Such a task raises numerous questions regarding the nature of the North American suburb at the beginning of the twenty-first century. For instance, where is this design methodology relevant? What are the criteria by which successful suburban design solutions can be judged? Or even, why is this important here and now? In addressing these questions and others, and by understanding what the desired product of suburban infill design should be, a clear design methodology can be articulated and architectural and planning controls can be established. An example showing the application of these controls and methodology will be presented at the end of the chapter.

The eight basic principles (outlined in Chapter 2) that can create a healthier, more sustainable suburban development—as well as a village settlement rather than a bedroom community—are a sound foundation on which to build a suburban design methodology (Van der Ryn and Calthorpe 1986). Depending upon the size of infill site, however, some principles become more prominent than others. In designing an infill community for 3,000 to 4,000 residents, for example, the justification for incorporating a new transportation system in the design is much stronger than if only a single suburban block were being redesigned. In the latter case, the strongest emphasis could instead be placed on designing at higher densities or building with more energy-efficient materials.

Another characteristic of the village-type suburb is its ability to function at various scales. Christopher Alexander et al.'s *A New Theory of Urban Design* (1987) stipulates that in designing a new centre as a compositional element of a development's "wholeness," three well-defined levels must be addressed. The centre to be designed (designated "centre X" in the thesis) must function at a scale larger than itself in order to support a larger system. It must also function at the scale of X, as developments adjacent to it function. And finally, centre X must function at a scale smaller than X, in such a way that smaller centres compose and support X. For the sake of clarity and applicability, this can be simplified by saying that a healthy suburb will function on a macro and micro scale. It follows that in order to guide the development of suburban infill at these two levels, the use of two separate codes is warranted.

Before the codes can be developed, however, the architect or planner must come to grips with the issue of context. There are several schools of thought on the manner in which context can be treated. Many designers would prefer to ignore built context in the hope of moving towards a new architecture that would solve all the problems created by the older environment. And some designers would address a site's context by creating contradictions and tensions between suburban fabric that is obviously old and suburban fabric that is obviously new. Perhaps the most sensitive (and most marketable) way of treating context, however, is to use the design articulations of the older community, augmented to address the demands of the present and potential markets. In attempting to socially integrate an infill development, a visual integration can only be an asset. The design articulations that can be implemented range from major built elements such as roof form, building typology, and porch/yard design to seemingly minor nuances such as ornamental grillework or masonry detailing. It should be stressed that the designer and planner are not merely replicating what already surrounds the design site. As seen earlier in this book, the demands that society places on the suburbs of North America at present differ tremendously from the demands that existed at the time of their original construction. The designer must therefore address the changed nature of the suburb, hopefully in a manner that is not an affront to what is already present.

The first step to be taken by the designer, therefore, is a thorough documentation of site context. Such documentation can take the form of a written or pictorial guide to the built elements that are perceived to be important in visually defining the community. Also, a study of the community's history and an investigation of the intended infill site's previous role in the community should be conducted. Though most postwar suburbs have not yet formed historical societies, such organizations can be valuable resources in investigating the character of older communities and receiving design advice. Also, the major civic, social, and religious buildings of the area should be included in the documentation of the site context. A profile of the current demographics of the community should be obtained from the municipality, as well as an index of local amenities and businesses. Supplementing this demographic and economic information should be the current zoning and land-use planning of the municipality.

At the larger macro scale, the critical regulating factors of the built environment are the zoning regulation and land-use plan. As seen in Chapter 4, these fundamental control mechanisms often restrict the built environment by limiting the community's ability to evolve in order to meet the demands of an unknown future. Daniels (1999) attributes such restrictions to sloppy zoning (meaning that there are jurisdictional contradictions, whereby local zoning may not be consistent with the comprehensive plan) or to ineffective and separatist zoning. Such zoning practices "separate rather than connect people." In *A Better Place to Live* (1994), Philip Langdon attributes weak planning to three causes. First, since urban planners work within a political system, they have become somewhat timid. By hesitating to "plan big," they retain their jobs though their ambitions are lowered, and when a crisis occurs, bold planning measures are rarely taken. Langdon also accuses planners of being influenced by commercial and business interests. And finally, rather than focusing on how regulations shape specific projects and holistic land-use patterns, planners look mostly at their planning process.

The first step in the new macro-level code, therefore, is to appeal to the municipal government for rezoning where applicable, in order to allow for a mixed-use, autonomous, local economy. This is a large, time-consuming step and one that would involve dealing with numerous levels of municipal governments.

Such a rezoning should be informed not only by what the emerging market dictates and the current zoning patterns but also by what had existed in the community before such zoning patterns. Such a rezoning harks back to the ideology of Jane Jacobs, who, in *The Death and Life of Great American Cities* (1961), proposed a reversion to the antiquated zoning patterns of the early 1900s to solve the ills of the modernist city. And though Jacobs's context is distinctly urban (her model being Hudson Street in New York City), the philosophy has an implicit intricacy and smallness that makes the idea applicable to suburban zoning as well.

An appeal for rezoning should be accompanied by at least a tentative sketch of the suburban design code that would govern development at the macro scale. The final version of the macro-scale design code should address several issues, both in writing and graphically.

First, it should address the built environment. Such issues as commercial-use location within individual units and in the neighbourhood, type of commercial activity allowed, and the percentage of unit area that can be dedicated to commerce should be specified. Residential building typology and neighbourhood location are other important aspects of built form.

Smaller but equally important issues should be specified next. These would include allowed building lot dimensions and configurations, building heights and placements, architectural elements (such as allowed percentage of openings on the residential and commercial facade), additions, and grow spaces. The design code should also address potential neighbourhood circulation paths for pedestrians and vehicular traffic. It should specify the acceptability or location of service lanes. Parking, whether on-street, indoor, or outdoor, also needs to be addressed. Streets in the infill site need to be designated for parking as double-sided, single-sided, metered, or no parking zones. Parking space configuration and quantity should be organized and integrated into the site planning and unit planning so as not to produce an eyesore and so that there is adequate parking for residents and neighbourhood businesses. Lastly, the problem of gracefully designating private open space (as opposed to public park space) should be considered. Specifications and dimensions of landscape buffers, as well as the heights and types of fencing permitted around private yard space, should be included in the code.

Having written a code that will guide development at the neighbourhood scale, the project architect can begin designing the units to be built at the infill site. It is beyond the scope of this book to suggest unit design solutions, but there are a few general rules that, when followed, will lead to the creation of more diverse, marketable, and sustainable housing. By attending to these rules, the project architect can formulate a unit design code and prepare an accompanying catalogue of architectural elements that are appropriate for use at a specific infill site.

Typically, developments are designed to attract buyers of similar socio-economic background. The unit cost and layout often lead to the same type of buyer, thereby creating a homogeneous community, rarely an accurate social cross-section. By introducing design principles that allow for easy alteration (such as eliminating interior load-bearing partitions) and for residents to work and live at the same location, a greater market sector, representing various income levels, can be attracted. Simply designing units of varying size and price can achieve the same result.

In order to decrease infrastructure costs and increase social intimacy, housing can be planned at greater-than-average density. By designing clustered or attached homes, we can encourage residents to interact with one another while enjoying the benefits of larger communal space. This social intimacy must, however, be balanced with residents' privacy and the greater ecological impact that such building density would have.

The micro-scale suburban design code should also be developed as a written and graphical code in which rules governing the appearance of the units on the site are accompanied by clarifying diagrams and drawings of built elements that can be used in the actual design of units.

The micro-scale code should address issues in unit massing such as building height and roof form, and smaller issues having to do with the character of the residential housing stock. The manner in which exterior social spaces (i.e., balconies, decks, patios, or any other additions to the front and rear) are integrated with units in the neighbourhood has a great deal to do with the quality of life that residents can expect to enjoy. If not carefully designed and regulated, these exterior elements can make an otherwise orderly and attractive neighbourhood seem chaotic and ramshackle. The same holds true for even smaller neighbourhood nuances like fencing, exterior stairs, or window and entrance door design. Special cases in the neighbourhood scheme, such as the articulation of corner units, should also be regulated in this code. Lastly, some regulation of the manipulations of interior partitions and spaces is necessary, both for structural reasons and in order to protect neighbourhood appearance from abnormal or erratic development. This is not to say that the ultimate goal of the micro-scale code is to create a homogeneous, conformist living environment. On the contrary, providing a catalogue of architectural elements by which a unit design is informed can establish a level of variety and heterogeneity while maintaining the character of the neighbourhood.

As a final exercise, which will help at both the presentation and design phases of project development, hypothetical situations involving temporal changes in the community and units can be created. Such an exercise acts as a check on what is to be designed, to ensure that it is widely applicable to the emerging markets. Such hypothetical developments can be used as a basis for guiding development of the infill in future years.

The Atwater Market Experiment

The Atwater Market experiment provides us with an opportunity to investigate the process of integrating a newly developed community into a well-established context. It also provides an opportunity to analyze the methodology that treats such a development on the macro and micro scales. In the course of this analysis, traditional notions of design are superseded, much as they have been in the previous two chapters, in that communities are recognized as dynamic entities, mandating considerations beyond the time when they are realized in construction and initial occupation.

The simulation that will be described here was executed under conditions that were as close to reality as possible. It is therefore possible, to a great extent, to treat this investigation as a template for actual development practice. From its analysis of the fundamental issues of the site and demographic trends to its actual design solutions, and in the resulting scaled codes, the issues that shape society were closely attended to.

The scenario centres on a developer who buys a plot of land in the heart of an existing community. The land—an open field—is to become the site of a new housing development. Because of the large size of the plot and low market demand, the developer wants to build the project in phases. He therefore asks a planner to propose a scheme that permits construction with the flexibility necessary to accommodate market changes of housing types and budgets. As a result of community and municipal requests and his own interest, the developer wants

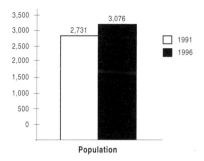

Figure 6.1. The population of the study site has increased by over 12% in a recent five-year period (after Statistics Canada 1999).

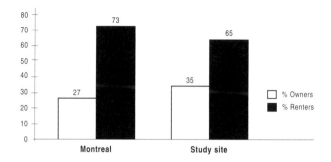

Figure 6.2. The study site has a higher proportion of homeowners than in the city of Montreal as a whole (after Statistics Canada 1999).

the project to fit in well with the existing architectural heritage and building style.

The Lachine Canal, which marks the southern edge of the site, opened in 1825 to become the access point to western Montreal for large shipping enterprises. In the mid-1800s, the Montreal and Lachine Rail Road Company built a route along Victoria Street to link the two municipalities, initiating the rapid industrial and social growth that continued until the early 1900s. At this time, the Lachine Canal, which had been the economic heart of the community, was superseded by the St. Lawrence Seaway and soon fell into disuse and disrepair. By the mid-1900s, the surrounding area (which includes the study site) was experiencing economic stagnation. This stagnation continued until only very recently, when the economy began showing signs of improvement because of a combination of factors, including the proximity to highways, a progressive urban plan, the rediscovery of heritage buildings, and the gentrification in the neighbourhood.

The population of the census tract that includes the Atwater Market study site has increased by over 12% in recent years (Figure 6.1). The proportion of anglophones to francophones in the sector is roughly one to five, the same as in the city of Montreal as a whole. People aged 30 to 34 form the largest age group. The majority of employed people work in service-sector jobs, with a minority in manufacturing and construction jobs. One in ten employed people work from their homes. The average income for men is $37,642, considerably higher than in surrounding sectors; the average income for women is $20,854, also considerably higher than in surrounding sectors. Even so, the incidence of low income among families is 33%, indicating a disparity between high- and low-income earners, a fact borne out by the recent gentrification of the neighbourhood (Statistics Canada 1999; Board of Trade of Metropolitan Montreal 1999).

The sector has a higher proportion of homeowners than in the city of Montreal as a whole (Figure 6.2). Well over half of the housing units were constructed after 1980. The average number of rooms per unit is 4.5, with an average of 1.8 bedrooms. The average unit price is $120,974, approximately the same as for the city of Montreal as a whole, but higher than the immediately surrounding sectors. There are a total of 1,560

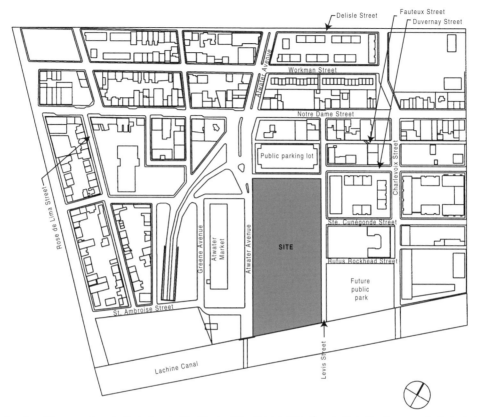

Figure 6.3. The site plan. The experiment site is located in Montreal by the Lachine Canal. Note its close proximity to both the Atwater Market and Notre Dame Street. Both of these are important community commercial centres that need to be considered when designing on the infill site.

households in the census tract, with single-person households making up the greatest number (Statistics Canada 1999; Ville de Montréal 1998).

The site on which this experiment was set is an old, abandoned train yard—a remnant of an obsolete economic sector. During the latter half of the last century, in many suburban developments across North America, when a form of transportation or production was superseded, the site was abandoned rather than rehabilitated. This was primarily an economic decision, and one that conflicts directly with Alexander's notion of building "whole." In this regard, the new North American technological economy presents an opportunity to bring these blighted areas back to life, by infusing mixed-use residential/commercial neighbourhoods into these vast, abandoned voids in the suburban fabric.

The infill site is located in Montreal, as seen in Figure 6.3, adjacent to the Lachine Canal. It is bounded on the west by Atwater Avenue and on the east by Levis Street. To its south is

Type of shop	Number	%
Antique store	37	44.5
Restaurant	12	14.5
Grocery store (general)	4	4.8
Furniture shop	3	4.8
Sink shop	3	4.8
Hair salon	2	2.4
Hardware store	2	2.4
Gas station	2	2.4
Travel agency	2	2.4
Copy shop	2	2.4
Grocery store (food)	1	1.2
Meat shop	1	1.2
Flower shop	1	1.2
Bar	1	1.2
Video rental store	1	1.2
Bicycle store	1	1.2
Key store	1	1.2
Electrical store	1	1.2
Tailor	1	1.2
Jeans store	1	1.2
Uniform store	1	1.2
Sports store	1	1.2
Chinese goods store	1	1.2
Massage	1	1.2
Total	**83**	**100**

Figure 6.4. Commercial activities located on Notre Dame Street. By indexing the identity and location of amenities in the existing community, a more informed decision can be made by planners regarding the amount and type of commercial space required on the infill site.

the canal, and to the north is Duvernay Street, just one block south of Notre Dame Street, a main commercial artery. An index of amenities along Notre Dame Street is shown in Figure 6.4.

After the site history and demographic/socio-economic trends were investigated, a thorough documentation of urban and architectural built form was made, resulting in an informative notion of site context.

There are several significant buildings close to the study site. These include a cultural centre, an elementary school, a daycare centre, and the popular Atwater Market, some of which are seen in Figure 6.5. The market will likely have the greatest and most direct impact on the site. With an area similar to that of the project site, the Atwater Market needs to be considered in terms of the problems that will be created by increased traffic circulation and noise level, as well as the problem of creating a sense of privacy and community in an area so close to this public fixture.

Issues having to do with unbuilt space should also be considered. The presence of parks greatly affects the livability of a residential development, as does the convenience and quantity of parking available. These two aspects of the existing community are documented in Figures 6.6 and 6.7.

Perhaps the most important characteristic of the neighbourhood in terms of developing housing stock within a context is the existing typology of built fabric. Traditional building

Georges Vanier Cultural Centre

Atwater Market

Ste. Irénée Church

Figure 6.5. Public buildings. In the immediate vicinity of the infill site, there is the Georges Vanier Cultural Centre (with a library), Ste. Irénée Church at the intersection of Atwater Avenue and Delisle Street, and, of course, the Atwater Market.

Figure 6.6. Open and park space. Six parks of varying scale are in the vicinity of the project, including a baseball field and two playgrounds. There is also a long plot of land adjacent to the Lachine Canal that has been designated for development as a linear park as the redevelopment of the canal area progresses. Residents of the infill project will have direct access to this park when it is finished.

Figure 6.7. Residential parking patterns. Residential communities to the east of the site provide on-site parking, located to the rear of the unit or in the basement. Backyard space is often sacrificed for parking if garage parking is not possible.

typologies found in the area, some of which are shown in Figure 6.8, are the duplex, triplex, quadruplex, quintuplex, and sextuplex. Apartment buildings and townhouses are the most typical residential building typology of this neighbourhood. Renovations in the area were apparent, as was new construction. Figure 6.9 shows several examples of newly built housing units. The more recent developments are apartment buildings of not more than three storeys, commonly articulated in the architectural language of more traditional building.

Corner units have a prominent presence in this area, traditionally incorporating mixed-use occupancies, with commercial enterprises at the ground level and residential housing in the floors above. Also, architectural flourishes such as elaborate balconies or roof forms are used to emphasize their importance. In new construction, however, mixed-use building is prohibited; subsequently the differentiation between levels is restrained, and any elaboration, in terms of materials or form, seems somewhat superficial. Figure 6.10 shows several examples of older and newer corner unit articulation.

In many units surrounding the infill site, a widespread mandate for increased internal area is articulated through the presence of balconies that have been enclosed, extra rooms grafted to the original units, and ground-level sheds. Figures 6.11 and 6.12 show several examples of these extensions. Such extensions are generally small and are used for storage or as a workspace. The construction and finish of these extensions is usually somewhat less precise than those of the rest of

the building and have a tendency to age badly. In general, such ramshackle extensions tend to be eyesores in the community.

Smaller architectural elements also need to be documented, as these are the aspects of design that will influence the catalogue of built elements contained in the micro-level code.

The windows that exist on site are generally large and rectangular. Special treatment is given to the masonry cladding of the building around the openings, in the form of special lintels and elaborate brickwork detailing. Some examples of this treatment are shown in Figure 6.13.

The finish of cornices on older buildings shows great attention in their detailing. They are generally made of wood and are painted a different colour from the rest of the building. In new construction, a variety of means are utilized to imitate this traditional construction. A few examples of cornice detailing are shown in Figure 6.14.

Entrance doors are also significant elements in the neighbourhoods surrounding the site. They are usually recessed in the wall and located under a balcony, which serves the dual purpose of providing cover and emphasis for the main entrance of the unit. Several examples of traditional unit entrances are shown in Figure 6.15.

In order to govern the community design, a macro-scale code was developed that embodied a strategy that would facilitate flexibility and provide users a range of options for responding to future growth and change in the community.

Figure 6.8. Typology of older built fabric. Adjacent to the site, there is a wide variation in building types. Duplex, triplex, quadruplex, quintuplex, and sextuplex are common, especially on Rose de Lima. The townhouse, two or three storeys high, is the most popular type of housing unit.

Figure 6.9. Typology of newly built fabric. Traditional materials and elements have been used in the construction of apartment buildings no higher than three storeys, duplexes, and triplexes. Mid-rise condominium housing is also present.

Figure 6.10. Treatment of corner units and mixed uses. Traditionally, corner units were treated with a balcony or prominent roof in order to accentuate their importance in the community as commercial sites at the ground level. Grocery stores, cafés, and restaurants are common in the area in mixed-use buildings. At present, no new mixed use is allowed by zoning.

Figure 6.11. Incidence and expression of extensions. Additions and extensions are common and take the form of ground-level, wood-frame sheds used for storage or workspace. They can also be raised to the level of the second or third storey and are often porches that were enclosed following occupancy.

Figure 6.12. Uses of balconies. Balconies serve both as exterior social space and as entrances for upper storeys. They are frequently enclosed when at the rear of the unit and used for storage or as an addition to the usable floor space of the unit.

Figure 6.13. Articulation of windows. On the body of the building, windows are rectangular with stone sills and a brick lintel pattern. At the uppermost floor, special treatment is given to the wooden frame of the window in a pseudo-dormer.

Figure 6.14. Articulation of cornices. Traditionally, cornices were ornate and painted, constructed of wood. In newer construction, these cornices are imitated with lower-maintenance materials.

Figure 6.15. Placement of entrance doors. On the ground floor, doors are set deeply in the masonry facade and are often located under the balcony of an upper floor.

Commercial use was designated for the basement and ground-floor levels of units facing Atwater Market and the Lachine Canal, as well as for corner units, in keeping with the spirit and traditions of the area. Residential use in the form of multi-family dwellings was specified for the rest of the development: rowhouses, semi-detached homes, condominiums, and apartments with building lot dimensions of 6 m by 30 m (18 ft by 90 ft). Unit density was capped at a maximum of one dwelling unit per floor. The complete macro-scale suburban design code is shown in Figure 6.16.

In order to provide coherence within the development, several guidelines were presented that governed the use of materials, percentage of allowable glazed opening per facade, roof slope, cornice detailing, and balcony extension. For instance, uniform height is specified for all building blocks along one street, in order to preserve coherence and maintain street perspectives.

The urban design code further lays out regulations regarding additions. Balconies, terraces, and decks in both the front and the rear of the units must comply with explicit dimensions, finishing treatment, and alignments. Exterior grow spaces are permitted if rear clearance exceeds 12 m (36 ft). And building extensions—vital in allowing for flexible use of the unit—are permitted but restricted to certain dimensions under specific clearance conditions.

As a critical element of the initial and progressive design of this community, circulation considerations received particular attention. This attention is hierarchically distributed from the broader scale of dimensions and routing to the narrower scale of suitable paving materials and landscaping treatment. Parking specifications were similarly explicit in specifying where on-street parking is permitted and the appropriate ratios between built area and outdoor parking areas. Parking criteria were further elaborated with quotas for vegetation, street furniture, lamps, and recycling facilities. Indoor parking was permitted in the basement of any building facing the street, provided detailing on the exterior complied with regulations regarding materials and colour treatment.

Public and private open spaces were also included in the urban design code and similarly follow a hierarchical establishment of guidelines. These parameters designate the appropriate dimension and composition while respecting both the public and private domains of these areas. For example, private lots must fulfill an 80% vegetation coverage requirement, and all landscaping is required to respect views from neighbouring properties as well as those from the street and public spaces. Guidelines legislating fence, tree, and hedge heights ensure the harmony of the development while providing a range of options that guide rather than restrict the users' choices.

Parallel to the macro-scale code, a code governing the design of units was developed (Figure 6.17), to maintain consistency with the overall design intentions of the community and, again, to allow for a great degree of flexibility throughout the development. A mechanism for flexibility is present throughout the specifications of this code. For example, the code specifying unit uses incorporates regulations not only for the family unit but also for the corner units and the specific option of including a home office. The regulation of the home office is further refined to protect the community at a broader level, by including specifications for signage.

In developing a catalogue of elements, the objective is to offer choice to meet the specific needs of the users and the opportunity for user participation in determining the appearance of the neighbourhood. This catalogue includes both abstract and concrete detailed requisite specifications for elements such as fenestration, entrance doors, fences, balconies, and parameters for expansion. Consequently, the harmony of the development is maintained, though there are numerous unique unit designs.

The scenario design of the community follows the code's philosophy in that it is divided into two sections according to scale. The exercise was done in order to facilitate progressive development and provide a foundation for future expansions that maintain the intent of the initial development. When the progression of the community development is examined, the intent to accommodate diversity and future modification is apparent at both the urban and unit scales.

Figure 6.16. Macro-scale suburban design code (after Ma et al. 1999).

The Built Environment

Commercial Use

▶ Permitted Locations

• Units facing the Atwater Market

• The corner units at the intersection of Levis and Sainte-Cunégonde Streets

• The ground floor and basement of units facing the Lachine Canal

▶ Permitted Commercial Uses

• In the units facing the Atwater Market: grocery stores, bakery, fruit stores, flower shops, barbershops, small restaurants and cafés on the ground floor; offices on any level of units

• In the corner units at the intersection of Levis and Sainte-Cunégonde Streets: dépanneurs and convenience stores

• Units facing the Lachine Canal: cafés and gift shops

▶ Percentage of Floor Area Dedicated to Commercial Uses

• Units facing the Atwater Market: 35%, and 15% for offices

• Units facing the Lachine Canal: 10% or less

Percentage of commercial uses

Residential Use

(all units other than described above are strictly residential)

▶ Permitted Locations

• Units facing the Atwater Market: all floors above the ground level

• Units facing internal pathways: all floors except basement when used for parking

• Units facing Levis Street: all floors except basement when used for parking

• Units facing the Lachine Canal: all floors except the ground level when used for commercial uses

▶ Percentage of Floor Area Dedicated to Residential Uses

• Units facing the Atwater Market: 35% or higher

• Units facing internal pathways: 100%

• Units facing Levis Street: 95% or higher

• Units facing the Lachine Canal: 90% or higher

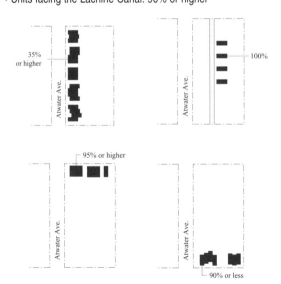

Percentage of residential uses

Figure 6.16 continued

▶ Permitted Multi-Family Building Typology

• Rowhouse

• Semi-detached house

• Condominium complex

• Apartment block

▶ Percentage of Multi-Family Dwellings at Time of Construction (modifiable later)

• One-floor units: 30%

• Two-floor units: 45%

• Three-floor units: 20%

• Four-floor units: 5%

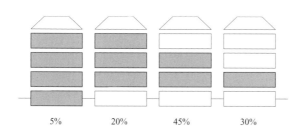

Percentage of multi-family dwellings

Street Cross-Section Building Mass

▶ On both sides of internal pathways, buildings should be of equal heights, not exceeding 3 storeys or 12 m.

▶ Other building heights must respect the height of neighbouring units and must not exceed 4 storeys or 16 m.

Building height of internal pathways

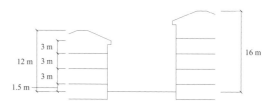

Building height of external pathways

Organization of Building Lots and Building Blocks

▶ Lot dimensions are 6 m by 30 m (this may include exterior parking).

▶ Intermitted building blocks are to be no more than 42 m in width and 12 m in depth.

▶ Semi-detached houses, rowhouses, apartments, and condominiums designed to follow the Next Home concept are strongly recommended.

Treatment of Street Perspective

▶ Uniform height for all building blocks should be maintained along one street.

Figure 6.16 continued

Building Height versus Street Width

▶ Building height must stand between 30 and 45 degrees when measured from the furthermost point of the opposing sidewalk.

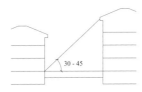

Building height versus street width

Building Placement

▶ Front alignment and setback should be within 3 m to 5 m.
▶ Side alignment and setback should be no less than 3 m.
▶ Rear alignment and setback should be no less than 6 m.

Unit Subdivision

▶ Maximum of one dwelling unit per floor.
▶ Typical dwelling unit dimensions approximately 6 m wide by 12 m deep.

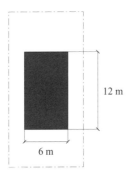

Unit subdivision

Grow Spaces

▶ Grow space is allowed only if the rear clearance between units is greater than 12 m.
▶ No openings are permitted on the surfaces along mitoyen line.
▶ Building extension maximum dimension is 3 m if only one facade is available for expansion; maximum dimension is 6 m if two exposed facades are available.

Figure 6.16 continued

Circulation

Service Lanes

▸ Service lanes are not permitted.

Pedestrian Paths

▸ Location of paths shall be within the landscaped area at the rear of units.

▸ There shall be only one pedestrian path running north and south on site.

▸ Width of path shall not exceed 2 m.

▸ Paving of the path shall be done in either brick or stone in a uniform pattern.

▸ Landscaping along the path shall include private lawns, trees, flower beds, benches, lamps, and garbage cans.

▸ At intersections with public streets, painting on the ground or a change in paving pattern shall signal pedestrian crossing.

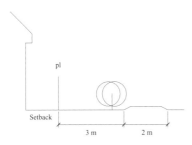

Pedestrian path width

Paving surface material: brick or stone

Traffic Paths

▸ Width of streets shall be 7 m.

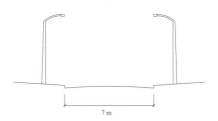

Vehicle path width

Parking

On-Street Parking

▸ On Atwater Street, parking shall be permitted on both sides and include loading areas for commerce within the community.

▸ On Levis Street, parking shall be permitted on one side of the street.

Outdoor Parking

▸ Area dedicated to parking shall be equal to 50% of built area.

▸ At least one parking space per dwelling shall be provided.

▸ Minimum parking dimensions shall be 3 m by 5 m.

▸ Service road design shall conform to Architectural Graphic Standards and Building Code minimum standards.

▸ Landscape buffer zones of at least 25% of the parking area shall enclose exterior parking lots; there shall be a minimum 3 m green band.

▸ There shall be at least one tree per three parking spaces.

Figure 6.16 continued

- Street furniture shall include lamps, garbage cans, and recycling containers.
- Bumps or median blocks shall be provided to confine parking areas, reduce traffic speed, and restrict vehicular paths.
- Minimum distance from parking to front and rear entrances to units shall be 30 m.

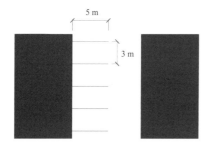

Minimum parking dimension (outdoor)

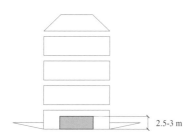

Garage minimum/maximum height

Indoor Parking

- Indoor parking shall be included in the basement of any building facing the street.
- Parking ramp design shall conform to Architectural Graphic Standards (Ramsey and Sleeper 1998) and Building Code minimum standards.
- Width of ramp shall be at least 6 m.
- Parking space dimension shall be at least 3 m by 6 m.
- Concrete surface of parking structure shall be protected with waterproof paint.
- Wall finishes of ramp shall be treated solid wood or artistic masonry block.
- Fire prevention devices shall be provided according to National Building Code.
- Garage doors shall be white.
- Garage doors shall not abut the street directly.
- Garage height shall be no greater than 3 m or less than 2.5 m, including structure.
- Minimum of 72 m^2 area for 3-car parking garage and 216 m^2 for 6-car parking garage.
- Minimum distance from parking to front and rear entrances to units shall be 5 m.

Figure 6.16 continued

Public and Private Open Space

Articulation of Private Space versus Public Space

▸ Minimum width of landscape buffer along sidewalk and pedestrian pathway shall be 3 m.

▸ Width of sidewalk shall not exceed 2 m or be less than 1.5 m.

▸ Open space (such as a mini-square/playground) shall be provided at each common backyard along with playground furniture (one piece per 10 m²), gazebos, statues, fountains, flower gardens, and trees (at least one per 18 m²)

▸ Lamps shall light sidewalks and pedestrian paths and be no more than 15 m apart.

▸ Trees of no more than 2 storeys high shall be planted at an interval of at least 10 m along the street and pedestrian path.

▸ Permissible tree species: hardwoods.

▸ At least one bench or garbage can shall be provided along pedestrian paths for every 18 m² of open space.

▸ At least one recycling container shall be provided in the outdoor parking lot.

▸ Public spaces shall be covered by at least 65% vegetation.

▸ Private lots shall be covered with at least 80% vegetation, excluding built area.

▸ All landscaping shall respect views from neighbouring properties, as well as to and from streets, porches, and public spaces.

▸ Swimming pools are not permitted.

One tree per 18 m²

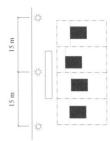

Lamps: 15 m apart

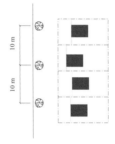

Trees: 10 m apart

Trees no more than 2 storeys high

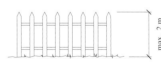

Wooden fence height

Hedge height

Unit Heights

▶ Units shall have a maximum of four floors, including a basement.
▶ Unit height shall not exceed 13.5 m or be less than 9 m as measured from street level to the highest point of the building.

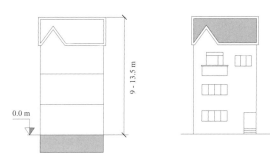

Minimum/maximum heights (metres)   *Maximum height (storeys)*

Unit Roofs

▶ Three varieties of dormer are permitted at roof level.
▶ The slope of the roof addressing the street shall be greater than 30°.
▶ The slope of the roof addressing the rear of the unit shall not exceed 45°.

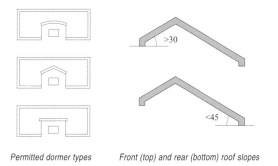

Permitted dormer types   *Front (top) and rear (bottom) roof slopes*

Articulation of Corner Units

▶ Units located at an intersection should turn the corner using a 45° angle in plan; the turned edge of the building should be 10 m in length.
▶ Special roof elements, such as a dormer or tower, shall be used to accentuate the special role corner units play in the community.
▶ The height of such accentuating elements shall not exceed one-quarter the height of a typical floor.
▶ Commercial signage must be placed at the chamfered corner of the corner unit, parallel to the wall.
▶ No perpendicular or neon signs are permitted.
▶ Balconies are permitted at the corner; they must be the same size as the corner cutout.

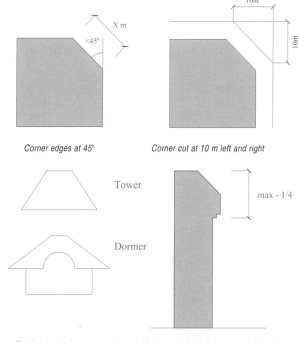

Corner edges at 45°   *Corner cut at 10 m left and right*

Roof elements in corner unit   *Maximum height of corner roof element*

Figure 6.17 continued

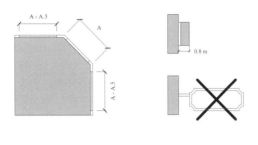

Commercial signage on corner unit   No perpendicular or neon signs allowed

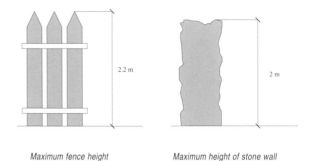

Maximum fence height   Maximum height of stone wall

Unit Fences

Fences at Front of Unit
▶ Front fences are not permitted.

Fences at Rear of Unit
▶ Fence height shall not exceed 2.2 m.
▶ Fence colour shall be white.
▶ Use of vegetation, such as flowers and bushes, to augment fencing is encouraged.
▶ Fences shall be constructed of wood.

Property Edge Boundary
▶ Stone wall barriers shall not exceed 2 m in height.
▶ Vegetation buffer zone shall be at least 0.5 m wide, with the property line lying at the exact centre of the zone.

Articulation of Architectural Elements

▶ Cladding material should be brick above the basement level.
▶ Brick finish should be smooth with tongued brick joints; no painting is allowed on brickwork.
▶ Area of openings in the facade should not exceed 40% or be less than 20% of the facade area.
▶ Cornice extensions should be within 0.45 m of the facade.
▶ Cornices should be constructed of either wood or metal and fit local context in design and colour.
▶ A maximum of one balcony, bay window, or French window is permitted on the front or side facade of each building; balconies shall be provided at each floor at the rear of each unit.

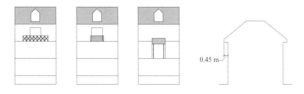

Number of balconies, bay windows, and French windows   Cornice extension

Figure 6.17 continued

Front Addition Articulation

▸ No front porches are permitted.

▸ Balcony maximum dimension: 1.2 m deep over the width of the unit; banister height shall not exceed 1.5 m or be less than 1 m.

▸ Balconies are permitted only on the upper floors of the unit.

▸ Balconies shall be constructed of metal or wood.

▸ Balconies shall be painted in a colour that complements or matches that of the other trim detailing on the unit.

▸ Balcony design shall be either rectangular or the combination of a rectangle and a curve.

▸ Landing maximum dimension: 1.5 m wide, 1.2 m deep.

▸ Steps dimension: width equal to that of landing; depth no greater than 2 m.

▸ Additions to be centred relative to their facade opening.

Rear Addition Articulation

▸ Balcony maximum dimension: 3 m deep over the width of the unit.

▸ If rear balconies are to be closed, they must conform to the standards for glazed openings of the front facade.

▸ Style, colour, and material of rear balconies should match those of the front balconies.

▸ Deck maximum dimension: 2 m wide, 3 m deep.

▸ Decks and terraces shall be constructed initially in pairs; one staircase shall service adjacent balconies.

▸ All rear additions shall be constructed of varnished wood or painted metal, in white or gray.

▸ Shed additions are not allowed.

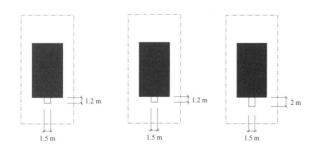

Front addition: balcony   *Front addition: landing*   *Front addition: step*

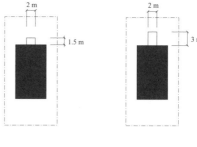

Rear addition: balcony   *Rear addition: deck*

Figure 6.17 continued

Exterior Stairs

▶ Units facing Levis Street are permitted to have external stairs.

▶ All external stairs shall have the same style and design.

▶ Stair design shall conform to the minimum standard specified by the most current Architectural Graphic Standards and local building code.

▶ Stairs shall not extend more than 3 m from the facade.

▶ Exterior staircases shall be of metal construction with wooden treads.

▶ The colour of exterior stairs shall complement or match that of the other trim detailing on the building.

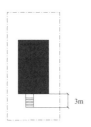

Exterior stair: front facade

Interior Alterations

▶ Adjacent units can be combined both vertically and horizontally.

▶ Attics and mezzanines are permitted with areas less than 40% of the total area of one floor.

▶ All interior partitions are non-load bearing and may be removed.

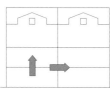

Combining units

Attics and mezzanines

Window Articulation

At the Uppermost Level

▶ All windows at the attic floor should have a decorative frame.

▶ Frame shape and design shall correspond to examples in architectural catalogue.

▶ Decorative frame should not be taller than one-half of the height of the window or shorter than one-quarter of the height of the window.

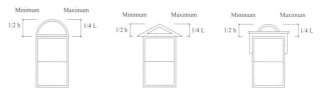

Window shapes and heights at uppermost level

At the Body of the Building

▶ All windows shall be rectangular and oriented vertically.

▶ Window height shall be no more than three-quarters of the height of the room in which the window is located and no less than one-half that height.

▶ Window width shall be no more than two-thirds of the height of the room in which the window is located and no less than one-seventh that height.

▶ All windows shall have a displacement greater than 1 m from all exterior walls.

▶ Window frame colour shall match or complement that of its neighbouring units' trim.

▶ All front facades shall have no more than a 60% area of glazed opening or less than 30%.

▶ No reflective glass is permitted.

Figure 6.17 continued

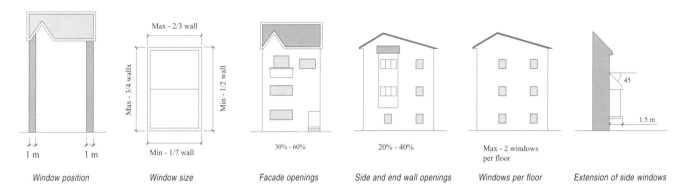

Window position	*Window size*	*Facade openings*	*Side and end wall openings*	*Windows per floor*	*Extension of side windows*

At the Side or End Wall

▶ Total glazed area on the side wall shall not exceed 40% or be less than 20% of the total wall area.

▶ No more than two windows per floor are permitted.

▶ Shape, colour, and dimension of windows on the side wall shall match those of windows at the body of the building.

▶ Bay windows are permitted only on the upper floors of the unit; if there is a basement, bay windows are permitted on the first floor.

▶ The maximum depth of a bay window is 1 m. The width of a bay window should be no greater than one-quarter the width of the unit exterior wall and no less than one-eighth that width.

▶ Bay windows can be no higher than two storeys or 6 m.

▶ Exterior cladding of bay windows should match that of the wall in which it is set.

▶ Bay window design should be rectangular or rectangular with chamfered edges.

▶ Bay window roof slope must be greater than 45° and may be constructed of transparent material.

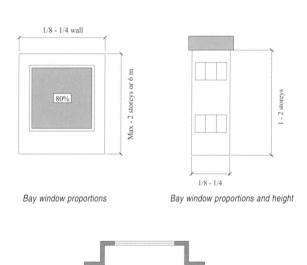

Bay window proportions *Bay window proportions and height*

Bay window shape

Figure 6.17 continued

Residential Entrances

▸ Width of the primary residential entrance shall not exceed 1.2 m or be less than 0.9 m.

▸ Height of the primary residential entrance shall not exceed 2.2 m or be less than 1.9 m.

▸ Primary residential entrances shall have an ornamental crown constructed of wood, brick, or glass and no higher than 0.5 m.

▸ Entrances must have recesses or eaves, the depth of which should not exceed 1.5 m or be less than 0.9 m.

▸ Residential doors shall be made of natural materials, such as wood, or of recycled material.

▸ Exterior door colour shall match that of the windows.

▸ Mailbox dimensions shall not exceed 0.25 m by 0.35 m and should be constructed of wood.

▸ Address signs shall be placed at the right side of the main entrance.

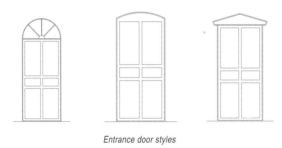

Entrance door styles

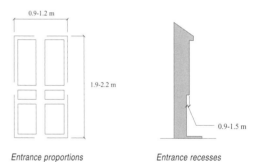

Entrance proportions   *Entrance recesses*

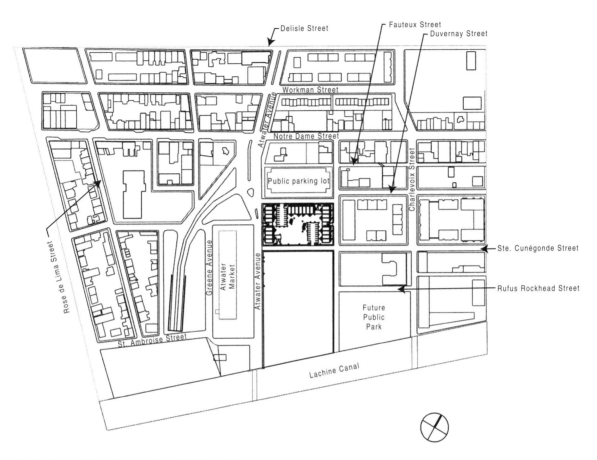

Figure 6.18. Site Master Plan, Phase I - Year 2000 (Lu 1999).

Phase I of the community design scenario is a temporal snapshot of the year 2000, shown in Figure 6.18, with a scenario in which there is a greater demand for affordable housing in the area around Atwater Market. The economic boost at the threshold of the millennium generates interest in the affordable homes market, and the Atwater Market district seems like an appropriate place for affordable housing, as it is expected to experience a period of renewal. This phase involves the development of seventy affordable residential units and eight mixed units geared towards buyers falling into the middle-income bracket who wish to own their own dwelling. Since Phase I is the primer for all subsequent development, its layout is a gauge of market response and an aid to the developer in determining the specific demands of constituents in the target market.

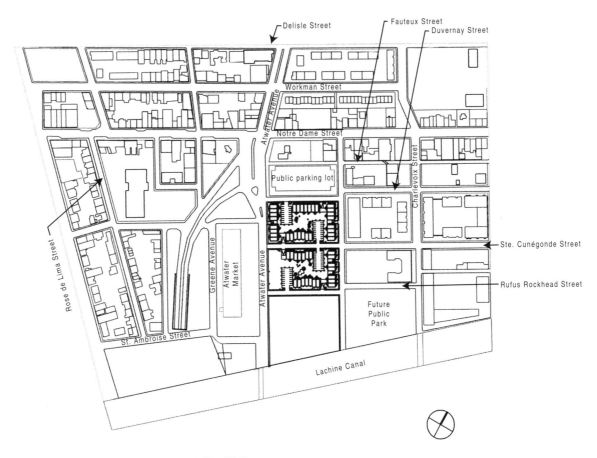

Figure 6.19. Site Master Plan, Phase II - Year 2003 (Lu 1999).

In the year 2003, the Phase II scenario of the community development is implemented. The site master plan at this time is shown in Figure 6.19. A rising economy attracts middle- to high-income real estate investors—the downtown periphery is in high demand. Proximity to the Lachine Canal parks, the Atwater Market, public transportation, and major highways causes increased demand in this area. A consistent, high qual-

ity of residential life in this developing area is also a major attraction. The demand for higher-end units has motivated a developer to build more opulent condominiums in the mid-price range bracket. Like Phase I, this development will also serve as an economic barometer for the developer and will guide the manner in which the neighbourhood progresses towards the next phase of its life.

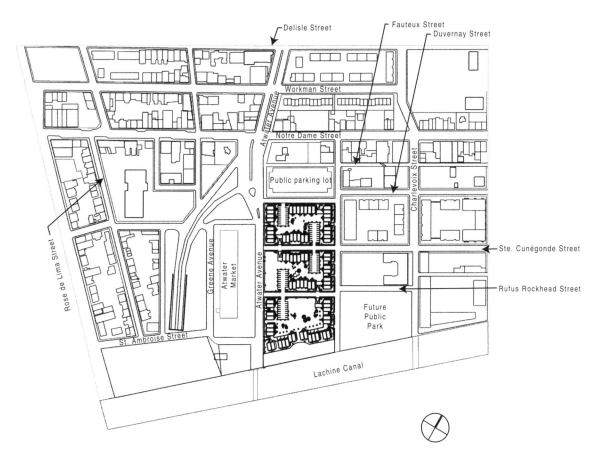

Delisle Street
Fauteux Street
Duvernay Street
Workman Street
Atwater Avenue
Notre Dame Street
Charlevoix Street
Public parking lot
Ste. Cunégonde Street
Rose de Lima Street
Greene Avenue
Atwater Market
Atwater Avenue
Rufus Rockhead Street
Future Public Park
St. Ambroise Street
Lachine Canal

Figure 6.20. Site Master Plan, Phase III - Year 2006 (Lu 1999).

Phase III, shown in Figure 6.20, occurs in the year 2006, the early retirement period of baby boomers. The dwellings are well finished and present high quality to this target market as the most expensive and luxurious units within the project yet. This time is ideal for luxury units because of the low turnover rates inherent in higher-priced homes and the fact that the intended consumer group is of retirement age. With the stratification of housing market prices spanning the three phases, a more heterogeneous environment is created that will ultimately remain healthy over the course of larger economic shifts.

In the final community design phase examined, the existing commercial structures on the site are demolished and a series

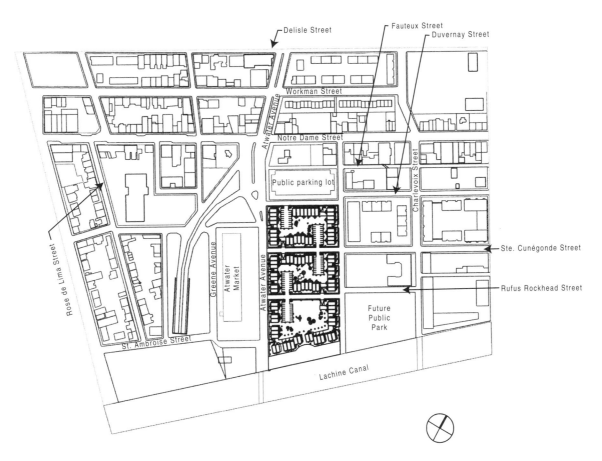

Figure 6.21. Site Master Plan, Phase IV - Year 2010 (Lu 1999).

of mixed-use condominiums are built in order to maximize the efficiency of the site. Phase IV is depicted in Figure 6.21. As the final opportunity for maximum exploitation of the site's potential and for the completion of the residential community, this development conforms to the sector where it is located. The levels of quality and price correspond to these parameters, and the

community is finished in terms of the initial macro-scale development.

The progressive evolution in the various phases of the community development is similarly carried out in the individual units. The following scenarios illustrate the advantage of designing flexible units and providing a mechanism whereby users can respond to their circumstances by modifying their living environments. The first scenario, in the year 2000, shown in Figure 6.22, examines a triplex in a row of similar plexes in a new development on an empty lot across from the Atwater Market. A real estate agent buys all three floors and plans to live on the ground floor and rent out the upper two. He takes advantage of the developer's offer to custom-design each unit for an additional administrative charge. The owner chooses an open concept for the front end of his own unit, where he places the living and dining areas and kitchen. He locates his bedroom with en suite study in the rear. For the second floor, the owner instructs the architect to design a one-bedroom apartment with en suite bathroom. He rents the unit to an unmarried nurse who works at a nearby hospital. On the third floor, the owner opts for a more traditional layout with a two-bedroom unit. After a short delay, he rents the unit to two university students. Within the first decade, this third-floor unit is rented again twice.

In the next simulation, shown in Figure 6.23, it is the year 2010. The owner of the triplex has decided to sell the entire building, having realized that he stands to gain more by selling each floor to a separate buyer. The purchasers of the ground-floor unit are an elderly couple who have just sold their single-family home in a suburban community. They want a pied-à-terre in town in addition to their small cottage in a rural area. They decide to renovate, and in the rear of the unit they construct an extension that becomes their bedroom. They

1st floor   *2nd floor*   *3rd floor*

Front elevation

Rear elevation

Figure 6.22. Unit Design - Year 2000 (after Tulupnikov 1999).

1st floor   2nd floor   3rd floor

Front elevation

Rear elevation

Figure 6.23. Unit Design - Year 2010 (after Tulupnikov 1999).

change the layout of the bathroom to create a more spacious area. The unit on the second floor is sold to a single, middle-aged buyer. She is an employee of a large investment firm and has recently moved to Montreal from another city. She, too, renovates: she eliminates a small powder room to make a large bathroom, and replaces the kitchen cabinets to create a more open space. The third floor is sold to a recently divorced thirty-two-year-old college professor. He changes the rear of the unit by demolishing the wall that separates the two back rooms. No significant changes are made to the front of the unit.

In the year 2020 (Figure 6.24), the elderly couple are still living on the ground floor and they decide to change the facade of their unit. They follow the previously established guidelines that formed part of their deed of sale and construct a bay window. The owner of the second floor, however, has been transferred to another city. In order to facilitate her move, her company buys the floor and turns it into a guest unit for employees who come to Montreal for extended stays. A year later, the college professor who owns the third floor is appointed to another university. His real estate agent finds a couple who have been looking for a large unit, so he approaches the firm that owns the second floor and arranges a deal whereby he can sell the second and third floors together to the couple. The couple engage in extensive renovations. They build an addition onto the back of the second floor, which they make their living/public space. They also change the location of the kitchen.

The stairs leading to the third floor become their private stairs. The third floor has space for a study at the front and a bedroom with bathroom in the rear.

By the year 2030 (Figure 6.25), in the final simulation, the husband of the ground-floor couple has passed away. The wife decides to move into an assisted-living residence. She sells her unit to a self-employed translator who uses a wheelchair and works from home. The ground floor is fitted to the needs of a handicapped person, with a new accessible bathroom and kitchen. The back portion of the unit is turned into a bedroom combined with a home office. The couple who live on the second and third floors still occupy the space. They have made no changes on the second floor, but they decide to add onto the rear of the third floor. They locate their bedroom in this new addition. They also renovate the bathroom and install a whirlpool bath.

The scenarios in the Atwater Market experiment were meant to illustrate that urban evolution has its own dynamics. The fitting of a new development with an existing community requires, first, an understanding of the established rhythms and patterns of the accretion over time and, second, the introduction of the new. The design guidelines were meant to provide the framework within which the new part would develop its own dynamics, in harmony with the old, for years to come.

1st floor   2nd floor   3rd floor

Front elevation

Rear elevation

Figure 6.24. Unit Design - Year 2020 (after Tulupnikov 1999).

1st floor   2nd floor   3rd floor

Front elevation

Rear elevation

Figure 6.25. Unit Design - Year 2030 (after Tulupnikov 1999).

In the past, new conceptual approaches to town planning have commonly been the outcome of necessary responses to societal needs. As demonstrated in the opening chapter of this book, visionaries such as Owen and Fourier attempted to alleviate the misery of urban dwellers by moving the working class from cluttered cities to more amenable conditions. Their proposed concepts were based on a new social agenda.

As time went on and the urban planning profession became more established, ideas and means of implementation continued to respond to emerging societal events. The development of post-Second World War suburbs, for example, was driven by the need to house many returning war veterans in an efficient yet comfortable manner. The increased size of the average home and the expansion of development standards were a reflection of economic prosperity in the decades that followed.

This book maintains that since it is difficult to predict future occurrences, we need to build greater flexibility into the design process. Trends and events at the dawn of the twenty-first century suggest that the future will be challenging to plan for. We are certainly justified in believing that we must think with an open mind.

The second half of the twentieth century was a period of significant demographic shifts. The decline in household size and the rise of the non-traditional family (singles and single-parent families) brought to the forefront the need to design homes that were different from those promoted in the preceding decades. Smaller households, at times with fewer means, led to renewed interest in smaller dwellings and, as a consequence, denser communities. The number of multi-unit dwellings increased. As society ventures forward, it is hard to say what our future demographic makeup will look like. Will the number of non-traditional households increase or will we return to more traditional family patterns? Will the drift to the suburbs continue or will the dense urban fabric become a strong attraction? Will there be new types of communities? Some predict the partition of large homes, others the building of more retirement communities and a rise in home (as opposed to hospital) care.

Suburban expansion has introduced another issue that will dominate planning concerns in the years to come: the environment. Scientists have confirmed the link between activities on earth and the effect on global climate. The subject has grabbed the attention not only of concerned citizens but of policymakers. Some argue that if significant action such as limiting emissions does not take place soon, the consequences will be beyond remedy. Over the past few decades, attempts have been made to curb the excessive use of depleted resources and to rein in urban sprawl. Densification and the need to shorten transportation routes and, as a consequence, lower air pollution and traffic congestion will no doubt be dominant planning issues in the years to come. Smaller homes at higher densities could be the result. Accordingly, housing density allowances might have to be changed. New densities could create communities of a far different character from the neighbourhoods built at present. Even on this topic, however, it is impossible to say whether or not the environment will continue to be a high-ranking concern. As other global issues such as world economic performance, hunger, and energy crises take centre stage, the environment could slip off the top-priority list on the international agenda.

Economic concerns have always been a critical part of design and development decisions. The cyclical nature of the North American economy has taught developers to modify their design offerings according to market fluctuations of prosperity or decline. Since most governments have bailed out of the lower-cost housing business, a wide affordability gap has opened up in many urban centres. The necessity of bridging this gap could certainly influence the housing agenda of many municipalities in the years to come. The need to lower land and infrastructure costs could lead to a movement to relax tough local bylaws that currently block the construction of smaller homes and narrower streets. This need to lower costs could change the course of residential design in some localities.

Economic trends have also led to the revival of home employment. Advances in digital communication have erased the need to work in a city-centre office. The home office has influenced and will continue to affect the way homes and communities are designed in the future. Old definitions and the segregation of home and work are likely to change. The introduction of different kinds of commercial activities into the hearts of neighbourhoods is unavoidable.

Planning and architectural trends are also instrumental in the requirement for flexibility in design-making processes. Over the years, numerous trendy design patterns have been introduced. Unlike the New Urbanism movement, for example, which has an ideological and technical spine, many of these new designs were conceived solely as fashions. The media have helped disseminate new housing models and interior patterns to countless viewers and readers. As homes continue to be sold, the tendency to implement new urban and architectural patterns will continue. Trends may well influence the overall design patterns of roads in a community or the homes built within them.

These societal changes will influence old and new communities and their homes. There is definitely a need for a decision-making structure that facilitates a process for dealing with these influences. This book has provided a detailed elaboration and illustration of three such situations: the metamorphosis of a well-established community, the design of a new development, and the insertion of new homes into an existing neighbourhood. Several principles guided the design for flexibility in all three cases. Regardless of the circumstances, these principles can be used in an open-ended design approach.

Familiarity with existing conditions is a precondition to any design process. The tendency is often to start with a clean slate, to ignore previous circumstances and history, and not to plan the future on the foundation of the past. Open-ended design, however, recognizes the need to identify trends to investigate precedent models in anticipation of events that may critically influence decision making. The vital signs would include socio-economic shifts and demographic changes. In the case of planning for the evolution of existing communities or building new developments in existing neighbourhoods, the urban and architectural contexts must be well studied. Such a study would range from street patterns and commercial amenities to door and window types. The resulting knowledge contributes to harmony between the old and the new.

Establishing a vision is the next step in planning for change. It would have to be the collective vision of a community, elected local officials, developers, and the planners themselves. A vision is a comprehensive portrait of what the community will become, regardless of passing trends. Will the community be made up of low- or high-rise buildings? Will it have large or small open spaces? Will it have heavy or light traffic on its streets? The medium that best represents the vision would likely be renderings and images of precedent models.

Developing a concept is the next stage in design for flexibility. Unlike in the conventional process, the planner would propose a conceptual approach to the patterns of arterial roads and the placement of homes, shops, and open spaces. As part of the concept, the planner would break down a large area into smaller sections to be developed in the future. During certain periods, such as an economic downturn, it would take a long time to construct a section. During times of economic prosperity and rapid expansion, more than one section could be developed rapidly.

The concept is to be accompanied by *guidelines*. Their role is to ensure that future builders respect the original vision, that despite changing events, constraints, and new opportunities, the eventual outcome will be true to the original concept. The guidelines have to be precise in their requirements but at the same time provide the flexibility and tolerance necessary to accommodate changes that arise from unforeseen occurrences. Their role is also to ensure that harmony will be maintained within a community over time as new sections are added.

An important final stage is the *simulation*. The objective is to test whether assumptions made in preparing the conceptual plan would actually work. By examining alternative design options that serve as demonstration models for the future, the planner would verify that the guidelines are not overly imposing and that they do not limit flexibility. The real test takes place once an actual development is constructed.

The evaluation of suburban subdivisions since the Second World War is mixed. On the one hand, they are no doubt popular places in which to live: almost half of North Americans have chosen to reside in suburban homes. On the other hand, the social and environmental implications of suburban living are in doubt. The built suburbs are here to stay, however, and new suburbs are under construction and will continue to be constructed across the continent. What we have attempted to do here is to propose a better way of contributing to the ongoing evolution of existing communities and the planning of new ones.

When a good conceptual framework is laid down—one that is complemented by design guidelines rigid enough to keep the evolution of a community in line with the original concept yet flexible enough to permit adaptation to unpredictable needs and occurrences—a recipe for a self-controlled process is created. As described in this book, an examination of the histories of some of the more successful North American suburban communities demonstrates that this has indeed been the case: a solid concept and flexible guidelines. The integrity of the original design concept has been preserved over the years.

Another ingredient, however, has contributed to the success of these communities: respect and discipline on the part of their builders and dwellers. Enforcement has not proven to be very successful in the past. It has frequently contributed to the very opposite reaction: disrespect for the law. Common sense and accretion created old European towns and villages that are admired today by all. And it is just such a model that this book has attempted to recreate, a model that values the old yet recognizes that shaping the built environment will require an improved and modified approach.

Abrams, Janet (1986). "The Room of the City: Two Projects by Andres Duany and Elizabeth Plater-Zyberk." *Lotus International* 50: 10.

Alexander, Christopher (1979). *The Timeless Way of Building*. New York: Oxford University Press.

Alexander, Christopher, Sara Ishikawa, and Murray Silverstein (1977). *A Pattern Language: Towns, Buildings, Construction*. New York: Oxford University Press.

Alexander, Christopher, Hajo Neis, Artemis Anninou, and Ingrid King (1987). *A New Theory of Urban Design*. New York: Oxford University Press.

Alnemer, Amar, Theresa Cheng, Benjamin Sternthal, and Dorota Wlodarczyk-Karzynska (1993). "The La Prairie Experiment" (design project). Montreal: McGill University School of Architecture Affordable Homes Program.

Anderson, George (1992). *Housing Policy in Canada*. Vancouver: University of British Columbia, for Canada Mortgage and Housing Corporation.

Anderson, William (1912). "Forest Hills Garden, Long Island." *Brickbuilder* 21, December.

Apgar, William (1991). *The State of the Nation's Housing 1991*. Cambridge, MA: Harvard University Joint Center for Housing Studies.

Architectural Forum (1949). 91, August: 86-87.

Architectural Forum (1950). 92, April: 136-37.

Artibise, F.J., and Gilbert A. Stelter (1979). "Planning and the Realities of Development." Pages 167-75 in *The Usable Urban Past*, ed. F.J. Artibise and Gilbert A. Stelter. Toronto: Macmillan of Canada.

Aston, Michael, and James Bond (1976). *The Landscape of Towns*. London: J.M. Dent and Sons.

Baine, Richard (1973). *Calgary: An Urban Study*. Toronto: Clark Irwin.

Baldassare, Mark (1986). *Trouble in Paradise*. New York: Columbia University Press.

Becker, Franklin D. (1977). *Housing Messages*. Stroudsburg, PA: Dowden, Hutchinson and Ross.

Becker, Franklin D., Stephanie Ashworth, Douglas Beaver, and Donald Poe. (1977). *User Participation, Personalization and Environmental Meaning: Three Field Studies*. Ithaca, NY: Cornell University Press.

Beecher, Jonathan (1986). *Charles Fourier: The Visionary and His World*. Berkeley: University of California Press.

Belgue, David (1994). *Les plans d'implantation et d'intégration architecturale: Guide explicatif*. Québec: Minister of Municipal Affairs.

Benevolo, Leonardo (1971). *The Origins of Modern Town Planning*. Trans. Judith Landry. Cambridge, MA: MIT Press.

Ben-Joseph, Eran, and David Gordon (2000). "Hexagonal Planning in Theory and Practice." *Journal of Urban Design* 5 (3), December: 237-65.

Board of Trade of Metropolitan Montreal (1999). *Trend Chart: Greater Montreal Region* 2 (1), August.

Brennan, William (1994). "Visions of a 'City Beautiful': The Origin and Impact of the Mawson Plans for Regina." *Saskatchewan History* 46 (2): 19-33.

Buckingham, James Silk (1849). *National Evils and Practical Remedies, with the Plan of a Model Town*. London.

Burton, J. Howes (1916). "Shall We Save New York?" *New York Times*, 5 and 6 March.

Canada Mortgage and Housing Corporation (CMHC) (1956). *Choosing a House Design*. Ottawa: CMHC.

- (1992). *Healthy Housing Design Competition Finalists*. Ottawa: CMHC.

- (1994). *Designs Produced for the Demonstration and Other Installations of Garden Suites*. Ottawa: CMHC.

Cherry, Gordon E. (1970). *Town Planning in Its Social Context*. London: Leonard Hill Books.

Choinière, Robert (1990). *Dossier socio-demographique et sanitaire*. Montréal: CLSC NDG/Montréal-Ouest.

Choko, Marc H. (1988). *Une Cité-Jardin à Montréal: La Cité-Jardin du Tricentenaire, 1940-1947*. Montréal: Méridien.

City of Montreal (1974). *By-law No. 1900, Building Code*. Montreal.

CLSC NDG/Montréal-Ouest (2000). *Statistiques et santé.* Accessed 4 April 2000: <www.santepubmtl.qc.ca/Portrait/Clsc/mtlouest.html>

Coffey, William J. (1994). *The Evolution of Canada's Metropolitan Economies.* Montreal: Institute for Research on Public Policy.

Colderley, Christopher (1999). "Welfare State Retrenchment and the Nonprofit Sector: The Problems, Policies, and Politics of Canadian Housing." *Journal of Policy History* 11 (3): 283-312.

Congress for the New Urbanism (CNU) (2001): *Charter of the New Urbanism.* Acessed 25 January 2001: <www.cnu.org/charter.html>

Congress for the New Urbanism (CNU), Kathleen McCormick, Robert Davis, and Shelley R. Poticha (1999). *Charter of the New Urbanism: Region/Neighborhood, District, and Corridor/Block, Street, and Building.* New York: McGraw-Hill.

Daniels, Thomas (1999). *When City and Country Collide.* Washington, DC: Island Press.

Dent, Laura (1993). "A Survey of Design Codes with Specific Reference to Contemporary Suburban Housing." M.Arch. thesis, McGill University School of Architecture.

Dirisamer, Richard, et al. (1976). "Project Dwelling of Tomorrow, Hollabrunn, Austria." *Industrialization Forum* 7 (1).

Dluhosch, Eric (1976). "Involving People in the Housing Process: The Story of Habraken's Supports and Detachables." *Industrialization Forum* 7 (1): 3-5.

- (1979). "Application of the Performance Concept to Facades and Balconies." In The Housing and Construction Industry in Egypt. Cambridge: Massachusetts Institute of Technology Adaptation Program.

Duany, Andres (1987). "New Town Ordinances and Codes." *Architectural Design* 71.

Duany, Andres, and Elizabeth Plater-Zyberk (1991). *Towns and Town-Making Principles.* Ed. Alex Krieger with William Lennertz. New York: Rizzoli.

Duany, Andres, Elizabeth Plater-Zyberk, and Jeff Speck (2000). *Suburban Nation: The Rise of Sprawl and the Decline of the American Dream.* New York: North Point Press.

Easterling, Keller (1985). "Seaside: Making a Town in America." *Princeton Architectural Journal.* Landscape Volume 2. New York: Princeton Architectural Press.

- (1993). *American Town Plans: A Comparative Time Line.* New York: Princeton Architectural Press.

Edwards, Arthur (1981). *The Design of Suburbia: A Critical Study in Environmental History.* London: Pembridge Press.

Elazar, Daniel (1966). "Are We a Nation of Cities." *Public Interest* 45, Summer.

Emodi, Tom (1989). "Emerging Urban Space in the Suburbs." *In Metropolitan Mutations: The Architecture of Emerging Urban Spaces,* ed. Detlet Mertins. Royal Architecture Institute of Canada Annual 1. Toronto: Little, Brown.

Feagin, Joe R. (1989). "Arenas of Conflict: Zoning and Land Use Reform in Critical Political-Economic Perspective." In *Zoning and the American Dream: Promises Still to Keep,* ed. Charles M. Haar and Jerold S. Kayden. Chicago: American Planning Association.

Filion, Pierre, and Trudi E. Bunting (1990). *Affordability of Housing in Canada.* Ottawa: Minister of Supply and Services.

Fisher, Susan, et al. (1993). Unpublished M.Arch. design studio work from the McGill University School of Architecture Affordable Homes Program.

Fisher, Thomas (1991). "The P/A Affordable House Competition." *Progressive Architecture,* June: 73-86.

Fishman, Robert (1987). *Bourgeois Utopias.* New York: Basic Books.

Foran, Max (1978). *Calgary: An Illustrated History.* Toronto: James Lorimer.

Fourier, Charles (1971). *The Utopian Vision of Charles Fourier: Selected Texts on Work, Love, and Passionate Attraction.* Trans.

and ed. Jonathan Beecher and Richard Bienvenu. Boston: Beacon Press.

Friedman, Avi (1995). "The Evolution of Design Characteristics during the Post-Second World War Housing Boom: The US Experience." *Journal of Design History* 8 (2): 131-46.

- (1996). "Flexible Planning Strategies: The La Prairie Experiment." *Plan Canada* 36 (2): 33-42.

- (1997a). "Design for Flexibility and Affordability: Learning from the Post-War Home." *Journal of Architectural Planning and Research* 14 (2), Summer: 150-70.

- (1997b). "Design for Change: Flexible Planning Strategies for the 1990s and Beyond." *Journal of Urban Design* 2 (3), October: 277-95.

- (1999). *Le Village: Retooling for the Next Century*. Prepared for Renaissance Waterfront Associates, Cornwall, ON. Montreal: McGill University School of Architecture Affordable Homes Program.

- (2001). *The Grow Home*. Montreal: McGill-Queen's University Press.

Friedman, Avi, Vince Cammalleri, Jim Nicell, François Dufaux, and Joanne Green (1993). *Sustainable Residential Developments: Planning, Design and Construction Principles ("Greening" the Grow Home)*. Prepared for Canada Mortgage and Housing Corporation. Montreal: McGill University School of Architecture Affordable Homes Program.

Friedman, Avi, Jennifer Steffel, and Jasmin Fréchette (1998a). "Planning for Suburban Evolution." *Plan Canada* 38 (4): 35-44.

Friedman, Avi, and David Krawitz (1998b). "The Next Home: Affordability through Flexibility and Choice." *Housing and Society* 25 (1 & 2): 103-16.

Gans, Herbert J. (1967). *The Levittowners*. New York: Pantheon Books.

Garreau, Joel (1991). *Edge City: Life on the New Frontier*. New York: Doubleday.

Gehl, Jan (1987). *Life Between Buildings: Using Public Space*. Trans. Jo Koch. New York: Van Nostrand Reinhold.

George, M.V. (1994). *Population Projections for Canada, Provinces, and Territories: 1993-2016*. Catalogue no. 91-520. Ottawa: Statistics Canada.

Gilliland, Jason (2000). "Visions and Revisions of House and Home: A Half-Century of Change in Montreal's 'Cité jardin.'" Pages 139-74 in *(Re)Development at the Urban Edges: Reflections on the Canadian Experience*, ed. Heather Nicol and Greg Halseth. Waterloo, ON: University of Waterloo Department of Geography.

Goethert, Zakia (1980). "Housing for Low-Income, Informal Sector." In *The Housing and Construction Industry in Egypt, Interim Report*. Cairo: Cairo University.

Goldberg, Michael, and Peter Horwood (1980). *Zoning: Its Costs and Relevance for the 1980s*. Vancouver: The Fraser Institute.

Goldberg, Michael, and John Mercer (1986). *The Myth of the North American City: Continentalism Challenged*. Vancouver: University of British Columbia Press.

Gosling, David, and Barry Maitland (1984). *Concepts of Urban Design*. London: St. Martin's Press.

Greenberg, Kenneth (1989). "Suburban Intensification." In *Metropolitan Mutations: The Architecture of Emerging Urban Spaces*, ed. Detlet Mertins. Royal Architecture Institute of Canada Annual 1. Toronto: Little, Brown.

Gunton, Thomas I. (1979). "The Ideas and Policies of the Canadian Planning Profession, 1909-1931." Pages 177-95 in *The Usable Urban Past*, ed. F.J. Artibise and Gilbert A. Stelter. Toronto: Macmillan of Canada.

Haar, Charles M. (1989). "Reflections on Euclid: Social Contract and Private Purpose." In *Zoning and the American Dream: Promises Still to Keep*, ed. Charles M. Haar and Jerold S. Kayden. Chicago: American Planning Association.

Habraken, John (1976). *Variations: The Systemic Design of Supports*.

Trans. Wim Wiewel. Cambridge, MA: Laboratory of Architecture and Planning at MIT.

Hanna, David, and Wendy Charlton (1985). "Walking Tour: Notre-Dame-de-Grâce." Montreal: Notre-Dame-de-Grâce Community Council.

Hason, Nino (1977). *The Emergence and Development of Zoning Controls in North American Municipalities: A Critical Analysis.* Papers on Planning and Design 13. Ed. David Hulchanski. Toronto: University of Toronto Department of Urban and Regional Planning.

Hershman, Salo (1975). "Salo Hershman: Competition for the Design of a Residential Development." *Aleph-Aleph: Monthly Review of Israel Institute of Architects, Association of Engineers and Architects in Israel* 9/10, April/June. Ed. Harry Frank.

Hodge, Gerald (1998). *Planning Canadian Communities: An Introduction to the Principles, Practice and Participants.* 3rd ed. Scarborough, ON: Nelson Canada.

Holdsworth, Deryck W., and Joan Simon (1993). "Housing Form and Use of Domestic Space." Pages 188-202 in *House, Home and Community*, ed. John R. Miron. Montreal: McGill-Queen's University Press; Ottawa: Canada Mortgage and Housing Corporation.

House and Home (1952). "The Adjustable House." 2 (6) December: 114-16.

Howard, Ebenezer (1902). *Garden Cities of Tomorrow* (original 1898 title: *Tomorrow: A Peaceful Path to Real Reform*). London: Swan Sonnenschein.

Institute of Traffic Engineers (ITE) (1965). Recommended Practice for Subdivision Streets. Washington DC: ITE.

Jackson, Frank (1985). *Sir Raymond Unwin: Architect, Planner and Visionary.* London: Zwemmer.

Jackson, Kenneth T. (1985). Crabgrass Frontier. New York: Oxford University Press.

Jacobs, Jane (1961). *The Death and Life of Great American Cities.* New York: Random House.

Kalman, Harold D. (1994). *A History of Canadian Architecture.* Toronto: Oxford University Press.

Kostof, Spiro (1995). *A History of Architecture: Settings and Rituals.* New York: Oxford University Press.

Langdon, Philip (1994). *A Better Place to Live.* Amherst: University of Massachusetts Press.

Lesher, Richard, and George Howick (1983). *Background Guidelines and Recommendations for Use in Assessing Effective Means of Channeling New Technologies.* Washington, DC: National Commission on Technology, Automation and Economic Progress.

Letchworth Garden City Heritage Foundation (2001). *Letchworth Garden City Heritage Foundation.* Accessed 1 February 2001: <www.letchworth.com>.

Leung, Hok-Lin (1994). "Residential Density and Quality of Life." Lecture given in the McGill University School of Architecture Affordable Homes Program.

Linteau, Paul-André (1985). *The Promoters' City: Building the Industrial Town of Maisonneuve, 1883-1918.* Trans. Robert Chodos. Toronto: James Lorimer.

Lodl, A.K., and E.R. Combs (1989). "Housing Adjustment of Rural Households: Decisions and Consequences." *Housing and Society* 16: 13-22.

Lu, Richard (1999). "The Atwater Market Experiment" (design project). Montreal: McGill University School of Architecture Affordable Homes Program.

Lynch, Kevin (1981). *A Theory of Good City Form.* Cambridge, MA: MIT Press.

- (1984). *Site Planning.* 3rd ed. Cambridge, MA: MIT Press.

Ma, Wei, Masayoshi Noguchi, and Richard Lu (1999). "The Atwater Market Experiment" (design project). Montreal: McGill University School of Architecture Affordable Homes Program.

MacBurnie, Ian (1992). *Reconsidering the Dream: Towards a Morphology for Mixed Density Block Structure in Suburbia.* Vol. 1. Ottawa: Canada Mortgage and Housing Corporation.

Macfadyen, Dugald (1933). *Sir Ebenezer Howard and the Town Planning Movement.* Manchester, UK: Manchester University Press.

Mansfeld, Al (1975). "Al Mansfeld: Competition for the Design of a Residential Development." *Aleph-Aleph: Monthly Review of Israel Institute of Architects, Association of Engineers and Architects in Israel* 9/10, April/June. Ed. Harry Frank.

Marsan, Jean-Claude (1981). *Montreal in Evolution.* Montreal: McGill-Queen's University Press.

Marsh, Benjamin Clarke (1909). *An Introduction to City Planning.* New York: Benjamin Clarke Marsh.

Marsh, Margaret (1990). *Suburban Lives.* New Brunswick, NJ: Rutgers University Press.

Mawson, Thomas H., and Sons (1912). "City of Calgary General Plan." Calgary: Glenbow-Alberta Institute.

- (1914). *Calgary: A Preliminary Scheme for Controlling the Economic Growth of the City.* London: Batsford.

McCann, L.D. (1996). "Planning and Building the Corporate Suburb of Mount Royal, 1910-1925." *Planning Perspectives* 11: 259-301.

McInnis, Stewart, ed. (1987). *Housing in Canada, 1945-1986: An Overview and Lessons Learned.* Ottawa: Canada Mortgage and Housing Corporation.

Miller, Mervyn (1989). *Letchworth: The First Garden City.* Chichester, UK: Phillimore.

- (1992). *Raymond Unwin: Garden Cities and Town Planning.* Leicester, UK: Leicester University Press.

Miron, John R. (1988). *Housing in Postwar Canada: Demographic Change, Household Formation, and Housing Demand.* Kingston and Montreal: McGill-Queen's University Press.

- (1993). "Lessons Learned from Canada's Post-War Housing Experience." Pages 353-70 in *House, Home, and Community: Progress in Housing Canadians*, 1945-1986, ed. John R. Miron. Montreal: McGill-Queen's University Press.

Mohney, David, and Keller Easterling, eds. (1991). *Seaside: Making a Town in America.* New York: Princeton Architectural Press.

Morris, Earl and Mary Winter. (1975). "A Theory of Family Housing Adjustment." *Journal of Marriage and the Family* 37 (1) February: 79-88.

- (1978). *Housing, Family, and Society.* Ames: Iowa State University, Department of Family Environment.

Muller, Peter O. (1981). *Contemporary Suburban America.* Englewood Cliffs, NJ: Prentice Hall.

Mumford, Lewis (1961). *The City in History: Its Origins, Its Transformations, and Its Prospects.* New York: Harcourt.

National Association of Home Builders (NAHB) (2001). *Characteristics of New Single-Family Homes: 1987-1999.* Accessed 17 January 2001: <www.nahb.com/facts/forecast/sf.html>.

National Commission on Urban Problems (1973). "Restrictive Zoning." In *Housing Urban America*, ed. John Pynoos, Robert Schafer, and Chester W. Hartman. Chicago: Aldine Publishing.

National Research Council of Canada (1980). *Residential Standards 1980.* Ottawa: National Research Council of Canada.

- (1995). *National Building Code of Canada.* Ottawa: National Research Council of Canada.

New York State Building Code (1986). "Title 9: Executive, Subtitle S: Housing and Community Renewal." New York.

Olmsted, Frederick Law (1992). *The Years of Olmsted, Vaux and Company*, 1865-1874. Vol. 6 of *The Papers of Frederick Law Olmsted.* Baltimore: Johns Hopkins University Press.

Ontario Ministry of Municipal Affairs (1989). *An Introduction to*

Community Planning. Toronto: Ministry of Municipal Affairs.

Ou, Michael, and Veronica Zidarich (1999). "The Atwater Market Experiment" (design project). Montreal: McGill University School of Architecture Affordable Homes Program.

Oxman, Robert, and Rebecca Oxman (1975). "Robert & Rebecca Oxman: Competition for the Design of a Residential Development." *Aleph-Aleph: Monthly Review of Israel Institute of Architects, Association of Engineers and Architects in Israel* 9/10, April/June. Ed. Harry Frank.

Oxman, Robert, G. Herbert, and A. Wachman (1984). "The Hierarchical Principle and Its Architectural Application." *Journal of Architectural Science* 26: 33-38.

Pantelopoulos, Maria (1993). "Small Living Spaces: A Study of Space Management in Wartime Homes in Montréal." M.Arch. thesis, McGill University School of Architecture.

Parrot, K. (1988). "The Relationship of Household Characteristics and the Home Remodelling Process." *Housing and Society* 15: 56-59.

Parrot, K., and A.K. Lodl (1991). "Household Remodelling: A Step Toward Integrating Independent Research." *Housing and Society* 18: 77-86.

Parsons, K.C. (1992). "British and American Community Design: Clarence Stein's Manhattan Transfer, 1924-74." *Planning Perspectives* 7: 191-210.

Patterson, T. William (1988). *Land Use Planning: Techniques of Implementation.* Rev. ed. Malabar, FL: Robert E. Krieger Publishing.

Perin, Constance (1977). *Everything in Its Place.* Princeton, NJ: Princeton University Press.

Perry, Clarence (1929). "The Neighbourhood Unit." *Regional Survey of New York and Its Environs.* Vol. 7. New York.

Platt, Rutherford H. (1996). *Land Use and Society: Geography, Law, and Public Policy.* Washington, DC: Island Press.

Poapst, James (1993). "Financing of Post-War Housing." In *House, Home, and Community: Progress in Housing Canadians, 1945-1986*, ed. John R. Miron. Montreal: McGill-Queen's University Press.

Podmore, Frank (1906). *Robert Owen: A Biography.* New York: Augustus M. Kelley.

Popenoe, David (1977). *The Suburban Environment: Sweden and the United States.* Chicago: University of Chicago Press.

Rabeneck, Andrew, et al. (1974). "Housing Flexibility/Adaptability?" *Architectural Design.* February: 76-91.

Radburn Association Archives (1929). *Plan of Northwest and Southwest Residential Districts.* Fairlawn, NJ: Radburn Association Archives.

Ramsey, Charles G., and Harold R. Sleeper (1998). *Architectural Graphic Standards* (The American Institute of Architects). 9th ed. New York: J. Wiley and Sons.

Rios, Aurea A. (1995). "Post-Occupancy Adaptation of Affordable Single-Family Housing in Montréal." M.Arch. thesis, McGill University School of Architecture.

Roeseler, Wolfgang G., and Bruce W. McClendon (1986). "Making Zoning Districts More Effective." *Journal of the American Planning Association* 52: 83-86.

Rogers, Ian (1973). *Canadian Law of Planning and Zoning.* Toronto: Carswell.

Rowe, Peter G. (1991). *Making a Middle Landscape.* Cambridge, MA: MIT Press.

Ryan, S., and M.G. McNally (1995). "Accessibility of Neotraditional Neighbourhoods: A Review of Design Concepts, Policies, and Recent Literature." *Transportation Research Record* 29 (2): 87-105.

Sanderson, Richard L. (1969). *Codes and Code Administration: An Introduction to Building Regulations in the United States.*

Chicago: Building Officials Conference of America.

Schlaepfer, Matthias (1983). *Adapting Planning Principles to Promote Housing Transformation.* A report for Canada Mortgage and Housing Corporation. Toronto: Schlaepfer and Associates.

Schoenauer, Norbert (2000). *6000 Years of Housing.* New York: W.W. Norton.

Seek, N.H. (1983). "Adjusting Housing Consumption: Improve or Move." *Urban Studies* 20: 455-69.

Senbel, Maged (1995). "Working at Home and Sustainable Living: Architecture and Planning Implications." M.Arch. thesis, McGill University School of Architecture.

Sewell, John (1993). *The Shape of the City: Toronto Struggles with Modern Planning.* Toronto: University of Toronto Press.

- (1994). *Houses and Homes: Housing for Canadians.* Toronto: James Lorimer.

Shaker Village Standards (1928). 2nd ed. Cleveland: Van Sweringen.

Simpson, Michael (1985). *Thomas Adams and the Modern Planning Movement: Britain, Canada, and the United States, 1900-1940.* London: Mansell.

Smith, Lawrence Berk (1974). *The Postwar Canadian Housing and Residential Mortgage Markets and the Role of Government.* Toronto: University of Toronto Press.

Southworth, Michael, and Eran Ben-Joseph (1997). *Streets and the Shaping of Towns and Cities.* New York: McGraw-Hill.

Spelt, Jacob (1973). *Toronto.* Don Mills, ON: Collier-Macmillan Canada.

Sprieregen, Paul D. (1985). *Pre-Design 1+2.* Los Angeles: Architectural License Seminars.

Stapleton, C.W. (1980). "Reformation of the Life-Cycle Concept: Implications for Residential Mobility." *Environment and Planning* A12: 1103-18.

Statistics Canada (1994). *1991 Census Highlights as Released by The Daily* (Tuesday, 7 July 1992: "Age, Sex, Marital Status, Families, Dwellings and Households"). Catalogue no. 96-304E.

Ottawa: Statistics Canada.

- (1999). *Profile of Census Tracts in Montréal (Data Products: Area Profiles: 1996 Census of Population).* Catalogue number 95-199-XPB. Ottawa: Statistics Canada.

- (2000). *Statistical Profile Highlights: Montréal (Ville), Quebec.* Accessed 5 April 2000: <ww2.statcan.ca/english/profil/>.

Steffel, Jennifer E. (1995). "Storming the Suburban Fortress: Understanding the NIMBY Phenomenon." M.Arch. thesis, McGill University School of Architecture.

Stein, Clarence S. (1957). *Toward New Towns for America.* New York: Reinhold.

Stern, Robert M., and John Montague Massengale, eds. (1981). "The Anglo-American Suburb." *Architectural Design* 51: 10/11.

Stilgoe, John R. (1988). *Borderland: Origins of the American Suburb, 1820-1838.* New Haven, CT: Yale University Press.

Tatsumi, Kuan, et al. (1987). "Two Step Housing System." *Open House International* 12 (2).

Teasdale, Pierre, and Martin Wexler (1993). *Family Dynamics, Residential Adjustments, and Dwelling Adaptability.* Ottawa: Canada Mortgage and Housing Corporation.

Toll, Seymour (1969). *Zoned American.* New York: Grossman Publishers.

Tulupnikov, Ivan (1999). "The Atwater Market Experiment" (design project). Montreal: McGill University School of Architecture Affordable Homes Program.

Turner, Ralph Edmund (1934). *James Silk Buckingham, 1786-1855: A Social Biography.* New York: McGraw-Hill.

United States Bureau of the Census (1966). *Housing Construction Statistics 1889-1964.* Washington, DC: United States Bureau of the Census.

- (1999). *American Housing Survey: Detailed Tables for Total Occupied Housing Units: Table 2-1: How Many Homes Are*

There? Accessed 17 January 2001: <www.census.gov/hhes/
www/housing/ahs/99dtchrt/tab2-1.html>.

Unwin, Raymond (1909). *Town Planning in Practice: An Introduction to the Art of Designing Cities and Suburbs.* London: Adelphi Terrace.

USA Today (1995). "Work at Home." 29 June: 1B.

Van der Ryn, Sim, and Peter Calthorpe (1986). *Sustainable Communities: A New Design Synthesis for Cities, Suburbs and Towns.* San Francisco: Sierra Club Books.

Van Nus, Walter (1979). "Toward the City Efficient: The Theory and Practice of Zoning, 1919-1939." Pages 226-46 in *The Usable Urban Past*, ed. F.J. Artibise and Gilbert A. Stelter. Toronto: Macmillan of Canada.

- (1984). "The Fate of City Beautiful Thought in Canada, 1893-1930." Pages 167-86 in *The Canadian City: Essays in Urban and Social History*, ed. F.J. Artibise and Gilbert A. Stelter. Ottawa: Carleton University Press.

Ville de la Prairie (1992). *Zoning Regulations*, No. 645. La Prairie: Ville de la Prairie.

Ville de Montréal (1998). *Montréal Facts and Figures - Population.* Accessed 31 October 1998: <www.ville.montréal.qc.ca/urb_ demo/mtlbref/engl/mtlpop.htm>

Western Horticultural Review (1850). "Scarlet Oaks Cottage."

Westmount Architectural and Planning Commission (1987). *Building in Westmount: Criteria for the Design of New Buildings.* Westmount, QC: Westmount Architectural and Planning Commission.

Wolfe, Jeanne M. (1994). "Our Common Past: An Interpretation of Canadian Planning History." *Plan Canada*, July: 12-34.

Wood, Eugene (1910). "Why Pay Rent?" *Everybody's Magazine* 22, June: 765-74.

Wood, Paul (1984). *Site Design.* Los Angeles: Architectural License Seminars.

Wright, Gwendolyn (1981). *Building the American Dream.* Cambridge, MA: MIT Press.

Photographs

Avi Friedman: Figures 4.3 4.11, 4.12, 4.28, 4.29, 4.30, 4.31, 4.32, 4.33, 4.34, 4.35, 5.13, 5.14, 5.15, 6.4, 6.5, 6.6, 6.7 6.8, 6.9, 6.10, and 6.11

Rick Kerrigan: Figure 4.19

Wei Ma: Figure 6.8

Veronica Zidarich: Figures 6.10, 6.12, 6.13, and 6.14

Other Figures

Figure 1.8: Originally published in *The Suburban Environment: Sweden and the United States*, by David Popenoe (Chicago: University of Chicago Press, 1977). Reprinted with the permission of author.

Figure 1.12: From the 1995 edition of the National Building Code of Canada. Reprinted with the permission of the National Research Council of Canada.

Figures 1.15 and 1.16: Originally published in *Towns and Town-Making Principles*, by Andres Duany and Elizabeth Plater-Zyberk (New York: Rizzoli, 1991). Reprinted with the permission of the authors.

Figure 2.6: Originally published in *American Town Plans: A Comparative Time Line*, by Keller Easterling (New York: Princeton Architectural Press, 1993). Reprinted with the permission of Princeton Architectural Press.

Figure 3.1: Originally published in *A New Theory of Urban Design*, by Alexander, Christopher, Hajo Neis, Artemis Anninou, and Ingrid King (New York: Oxford University Press, 1987). Published with the permission of the authors.

Figures 3.2 and 3.3: Originally published in "Al Mansfeld: Competition for the Design of a Residential Development, " by Al Mansfeld, in *Aleph-Aleph: Monthly Review of Israel Institute of Architects, Association of Engineers and Architects in Israel* 9/10 (April/June 1975), ed. Harry Frank. Published with the permission of Association of Engineers and Architects in Israel.

Figure 3.4: Originally published in "Salo Hershman: Competition for the Design of a Residential Development," by Salo Hershman, in *Aleph-Aleph: Monthly Review of Israel Institute of Architects, Association of Engineers and Architects in Israel* 9/10 (April/June 1975), ed. Harry Frank. Published with the permission of Association of Engineers and Architects in Israel.

Figure 4.20: From *Designs Produced for the Demonstration and Other Installations of Garden Suites* (Ottawa: CMHC, 1994). Published with the permission of the Canada Mortgage and Housing Corporation.

Figure 5.2: Originally published in "Robert & Rebecca Oxman: Competition for the Design of a Residential Development," by Robert Oxman and Rebecca Oxman, in *Aleph-Aleph: Monthly Review of Israel Institute of Architects, Association of Engineers and Architects in Israel* 9/10 (April/June 1975), ed. Harry Frank. Published with the permission of Association of Engineers and Architects in Israel.

Index

design guidelines, 18f
design reviews, 18f, 20
of early urban reformers, 3-12
and extent of change in suburbs, 34
house specifications and mortgage approval, 32-33
knowledge of, first step in planning process, 54-55
land subdivision control, 18, 101
necessitated by Industrial Revolution, 3, vii
See also Zoning

Deed restrictions
     as control mechanism, 18f, 19-20
     in La Prairie simulation, 124, 127f-130f
Depression, Great
     and housing assistance in U.S., 28-29
Design codes
     and New Urbanists, 49
     for Seaside (Florida), 21-22, 23f, 24
     See also Design codes, neighbourhood (macro-level); Design
          codes, unit (micro-level)
Design codes, neighbourhood (macro-level)
     Atwater Market Experiment (Montreal), 145, 150, 151, 152f-157f
     for change in existing communities, 53f, 56-57
     in hierarchical planning process, 107-8, 124, 131f, 132f-133f
     infill designs, 136-38
     La Prairie simulation, 120, 123f, 124, 125f-129f, 132f-133f
     for mature community (NDG), 71-72, 73f-77f, 78
     Notre-Dame-de-Grâce simulation (Montreal), 71-72, 73f-77f, 78
Design codes, unit (micro-level)
     Atwater Market Experiment (Montreal), 151, 158f-163f
     infill designs, 138-39
     La Prairie subdivision simulation, 130f, 134f
Design process, for communities
     basic principles, 175-76

changes in last 50 years, 174
     need for densification of existing communities, 174
     as predictions for future difficult, 173
     required by economic concerns and trends, 174
     See also entries beginning with Planning
Design reformers. *See* Reformers of urban design
Design reviews, as control mechanism, 18f, 20
"Districting," 12
     See also Zoning
Diversity of neighbourhoods
     and Federal Housing Administration policies, 29
Don Mills (Ontario), postwar development, 31-32
Duany, Andres, 20-21

"**E**dge cities," 35
Emodi, Thomas, 42
Environment
     impact of urban sprawl, 174
     sustainable development principles for suburbia, 36-37

Federal Housing Administration (FHA) (U.S., 1934), 29-30, 32
Flexabilt Home, 78, 79f
Flexible design, houses
     Cape Cod floor plan, 32f, 33
     Flexabilt Home, 78, 79f
     modification scenarios in Atwater Market Experiment (Montreal),
          167-70, 168f-171f
     unit design code in Atwater Market Experiment (Montreal), 151,
          158f-163f
     unit design codes (micro-level), 136-39
Flexible design codes. *See* Design codes, neighbourhood (macro-
          level); Design codes, unit (micro-level); Design process,
          for communities
Flexible design process for communities. *See* Design process, for

communities
Forest Hill Gardens (New York), Garden Suburb, 9
Fourier, Charles, 3-4, 5f

Garden Cities
    Letchworth (England), 8-9, 10f
    and social concerns, 8
Garden Cities of Tomorrow (Howard, 1902), 8
Garden Suburbs
    Forest Hill Gardens (New York), 9
    Levittown (Pennsylvania), 11-12, 31, 33f
    Radburn (New Jersey), 10-11
    RPA (Regional Planning Association), 10
    variant of Garden City, 9
"Garden suites." *See* Ancillary units
Gosselin, Auguste, 34
"Granny flats." *See* Ancillary units
Great Depression. *See* Depression, Great

Haifa (Israel)
    Oxmans' hierarchical residential development, 101, 102f
    Shaar Ha'aliya community design, 44, 46f
Heights of Buildings Commission (New York City), 13
Hershman, Salo
    approach to incremental growth and flexibility, 43-44, 47f, 48
Hierarchical characterization
    concept in mass housing theory, 100-101
    in experimental development (*see* La Prairie [Quebec])
    in Oxmans' Haifa residential development, 101, 102f
    in traditional cities, 99-100
    in traditional suburbs, 100
    See also Planning process, hierarchical
Home offices
    in Notre-Dame-de-Grâce experiment (Montreal), 74f

scenario, ancillary unit construction, 96, 97f
scenarios, in-house alterations, 90, 91f, 92, 93f
trend due to economy, 174
Homeowners Loan Corporation (HOLC) (U.S., 1933), 28
Hoover, Herbert, 14
Housing stock
    housing starts post-WWI, 28
    housing starts post-WWII, 29-30, 31
    and large-scale builders post-WWII, 29-30
    prefabrication post-WWII, 32
    tract development (early 1900s), 27-28, 31
Howard, Ebenezer, 8-9

Industrial Revolution
    and urban outgrowth (suburbia), 3, 25-26, vii
Infill designs. *See* Planning process, infill design
Interstate Highway Act, impact on public transportation, 30

La Prairie (Quebec), experiment in development
    demographics of La Prairie, 113-14
    description of La Prairie, 111-14
    general approval process for all development, 116-17
    housing types in La Prairie, 113-14, 114f
    industrial park location, 116-17
    master plan of La Prairie, 114-16
    site, applicable zoning bylaws, 117, 118f
    site, vision of community, 120, 124
    site analysis, 117, 119f
    site circulation and parking, 125f, 126f, 128f, 132f-133f
    site description, 112f, 114, 114f
    site design code, 120, 124, 125f
    site design concept, 117, 122f
    site design flexibility, 120, 124
    site design plan, 120, 124

inefficient land utilization, 33-34

Van der Ryn, Sim, 36
Veterans Administration and mortgage guarantees, 29-30, 32
"Village settlement," 36

Wascana Centre (Saskatchewan), 6
Welwyn Garden City (England), 9
"Wholeness" concept of unified growth, 40-41
World War I
    postwar move to suburbia, 28
World War II
    postwar housing demand, 29-30, 31
Wright, Henry, 10

Zoning
    city plan required (in Canada), 14
    cumulative or pyramid zoning, 15
    definition, 15, 17
    "districting," 12
    early types, 12-14
    growth in Canada, 14-15
    knowledge of, first step in planning process, 54-55
    and land speculation, 15-16
    modification, methods for, 17-18
    multiple-use designations, 23f
    in New York City (early 1900s), 13-14
    proposed for mature community (NDG), 63, 64f, 65
    in Seaside (Florida), 21-22, 23f, 24
    in sector 102, Notre-Dame-de-Grâce (Montreal), 63, 64f, 65
    Standard State Enabling Act (U.S., 1924), 14
    stultifying and rigid in current period of change, 17, 52-53
    and subdivision control, 101
    supporters of, 14

as urban planning tool, 12, 17
zoning map, 15, 16f
See also Control mechanisms for growth

Set in Helvetica Narrow by Leon Phillips

Printed and bound in Canada by Friesens

Designer: Leon Phillips

Copy editor: Francis M. Chow

Proofreader: Andrea Kwan

Indexer: Patricia Buchanan